WOODSTOCK
SCHOLARSHIP

Woodstock Scholarship

An Interdisciplinary
Annotated Bibliography

Jeffrey N. Gatten

OpenBook Publishers

https://www.openbookpublishers.com

Loyola Marymount University has generously contributed towards the publication of this Open Access volume.

ISBN Paperback: 978-1-78374-288-2
ISBN Hardback: 978-1-78374-289-9
ISBN Digital (PDF): 978-1-78374-290-5
ISBN Digital ebook (epub): 978-1-78374-291-2
ISBN Digital ebook (mobi): 978-1-78374-292-9
DOI: 10.11647/OBP.0105

Cover image: John Flannery, *Woodstock* (2012). CC BY-SA 2.0, https://www.flickr.com/photos/drphotomoto/6857539392

All paper used by Open Book Publishers is SFI (Sustainable Forestry Initiative), PEFC (Programme for the Endorsement of Forest Certification Schemes) and Forest Stewardship Council(r)(FSC(r) certified.

Printed in the United Kingdom, United States, and Australia
by Lightning Source for Open Book Publishers (Cambridge, UK)

Contents

Preface

Since August 1969, the Woodstock Music and Art Fair looms large when recounting the history and impact of the baby boom generation and the societal upheavals of the Sixties. Scholars study the sociological, political, musical, and artistic impact of the event and use it as a cultural touchstone when exploring alternative perspectives or seeking clarity.

Scholarship is defined here as any work providing a serious treatment of the subject with the intent to inform, enlighten, educate, or add to a body of knowledge. Readers will find most items included are primarily interpretive and analytical, rather than merely descriptive. This, then, excludes most news publications tending to report on current events without attempting in-depth analysis (e.g., *Time*, *Newsweek*, *People*), popular reading materials (e.g., *Rolling Stone*), and reviews. Dissertations have been excluded due to being unpublished works. However, in an attempt to be more inclusive than exclusive, notable exceptions have been made in almost every genre. The Woodstock legacy continues and has a direct lineage manifested through anniversary events: Woodstock '79, Woodstock '89, Woodstock '94, and Woodstock '99. Therefore, selected scholarship on these happenings can be found within this work.

Chapters are organized into subject disciplines. Books, book chapters, journal articles, proceedings, videos, websites, transcriptions, and sound recordings are included when appropriate. Each entry contains bibliographic information applicable to the physical/digital format. Annotations are written to provide clear descriptive explanations of content. Each entry is numbered sequentially and identified in the authors/editors/directors and subject indexes by the entry number. The detailed indexes are designed to serve as the primary locating tools for this publication.

Woodstock scholarship does not stand alone as field of study, but it is at the cross-roads of a number of disciplines — music, history, cultural studies, sociology, arts and literature, media studies, politics and economics. This interdisciplinary annotated bibliography should facilitate research and study by students, scholars, teachers, and librarians in all these areas, as well as anyone seeking a deeper understanding of both the Woodstock Music and Art Fair phenomenon and the confluence of music, commerce and politics.

Bibliographies are works in progress which need constant updating as new resources become available. Therefore, in parallel with this edition is issued a free, socially enhanced version of *Woodstock Scholarship*. This socially editable version of the work is available on Wikiversity, a Wikimedia Foundation project devoted to educational resources. You are encouraged to help develop this collaborative edition by adding new entries and creating links to existing resources. You can access this online version via https://www.openbookpublishers.com/isbn/9781783742882#resources

I want to acknowledge and thank the libraries at California Institute of the Arts (CalArts) and Loyola Marymount University for providing access to many of these resources and for their overall efforts and support. This book is dedicated to Raida Gatten for her unwavering encouragement of anything and everything I undertake.

Introduction

The importance of the Woodstock Music and Art Fair cannot be overstated. Three days of music on a New York farm in August 1969 generated an ethos and a mythology (Denisoff, 1986); but was it merely a media contrivance? Depends upon who is asked. The importance is self-evident; the reason is elusive.

Throughout the 1960s, popular music became increasingly reflective and suggestive of the rising political and social consciousness of the youth culture. Examples can be seen in the development of the protest song genre within the folk music boom of the early Sixties and the marriage of lifestyle to music first reflected by The Beatles with fashion, followed by psychedelic music with the emerging drug culture. Woodstock was where these themes coalesced, thus becoming the "defining and last great moment of the 1960s" (Bennett, 2004). However, Woodstock also represented, in the same instance, an abundant amount of "experiences and ideas and moments" (Street, 2012). Thus, when exploring the complicated accounts and numerous facets of America during the turbulent Sixties one discovers scholarship on the key subjects, such as the Vietnam War or the Civil Rights Movement, often considering and debating the importance, relevance, and epic nature of Woodstock. Multiple narratives emerge: a radical engagement of the hippie movement, an overt commercial exploitation of youth culture, a political statement (Street, 2012).

Jimi Hendrix's performance provides just one example of the complexities encountered when trying to reach a definitive understanding of the Woodstock Music and Art Fair. A lot of ink has been used to analyze Hendrix's performance, a lot of ink. His

     http://dx.doi.org/10.11647/OBP.0105.07

rendition of "The Star Spangled Banner" at the event mattered to others in significant ways—artistically, socially, and politically.[1] Hendrix delivered one of the most important rock performance in the history of popular culture (Diltz, 2006). Floyd (1995) describes his execution style coming from the "practice and proclivities of numerous ancient and modern African and African-American music makers." Murray (1989) offers Hendrix's recital as "a compelling musical allegory of a nation tearing itself apart." Clarke (2005) provides a second-by-second breakdown of the performance, describing musical notes and their rendering throughout the performance, claiming nationalism and counterculture are both "simultaneously and antagonistically specified in the sounds of the performance." Others attempt to insert intent into the act which was "informed by a Zeitgeist and part of a larger critique of American involvement in the Vietnam War" (Fast and Pegley, 2012).

When asked directly why he chose to perform "The Star Spangled Banner" at Woodstock, Hendrix himself responded only with, "Oh, because we're all Americans. We're all Americans, aren't we? It was written and played in a very beautiful way, what they call a beautiful state. Nice, inspiring, your heart throbs, and you say, 'Great. I'm American.' But nowadays when we play it, we don't play it to take away all this greatness that America is supposed to have. We play it the way the air is in America today. The air is slightly static, isn't it?" (Steven, 2010). This seems to fall short of being a "stunning political critique" (Waksman, 2011) or moreover a dismantling of "the central ideas and mythologies of the United States" (Bass, 2002).

When it comes to the Woodstock Music and Art Fair, perception is everything. Popular music is created and managed by the music industry and acquires meaning through consumption (Street, 1986). Woodstock is often viewed cynically as just another manifestation of commercialism. Yet, to the more radical members of the 1960s counterculture, it was viewed as the beginning of a utopian political youth movement that, ultimately, was short-lived (Anderson, 1995). Woodstock may have provided a visualization of a primitive tribal bonding lifestyle, but the event did not, in fact, signal a cultural paradigm shift in any direction (Fischer, 2006). But how close did such a shift come

---

1   A recording of the performance is available at https://www.youtube.com/watch?v f=TKAwPA14Ni4

to being realized? If the festival had continued indefinitely, would a social order similar to contemporary society have established itself with capitalistic mechanisms, policing rules, and corrupt citizens (Howard, 1980)? While attending the Woodstock concert likely conveyed one was opposed to the Vietnam War, favored the legalization of marijuana, and supported the Civil Rights Movement, the expression did not develop into a permanent movement because there was a lack of leaders willing to establish an ideology and transform the energy of the event into political action (Rahman, 1996). "Perhaps it is asking too much of such a heterogeneous set of events to display a great deal of coherence—or, at least, to display a coherent philosophy of life, of action, or even art." (Moore, 2004).

The contexts surrounding the Woodstock Music and Art Fair paralleled the larger American cultural wars of the 1960s: the difficulties the festival promoters had in securing a site for the event and their successful and unsuccessful efforts at fostering positive community relations to that end; the local political maneuvering used in attempts to stop the concert; the local and state impact of the festival on elections, the legal system, and on legislation designed to prevent future large-scale events unless all issues of health, food, sanitation, crowd control, and safety were addressed; how the festival was viewed at the time in moral terms, by both proponents and opponents (Helfrich, 2010). Each instance a case study in the youth movement and the pushback from the establishment, liberalism versus conservativism, and socialism versus capitalism.

Historical texts consider Woodstock as a series of discreet events: the story of how Joel Rosenmann, John Roberts, Artie Kornfeld, and Michael Lang (the four promoters of the festival) came to form Woodstock Ventures; securing a site which eventually leads to a meeting with farmer/businessman Max Yasgur; managing the event as a series of last minute activities and the consequences regarding traffic control, food, and security arrangements; surviving the weather; facing post-event financial issues and the eventual success of the motion picture *Woodstock* (Brant, 2008). Chronicled are rich personal accounts from individuals who attended, performed, or worked the festival, offering unique and insightful perspectives on the phenomenon. Typically, treatises conclude with a discussion of the impact on the music industry, performers, and subsequent music festivals. Often included are appended discussions devoted to Woodstock '79, Woodstock '89, Woodstock '94, and Woodstock '99. Other texts place Woodstock within the larger context of 1960s America (e.g., the rise of a counterculture) and the role of music in shaping society during that time period (e.g., Bob Dylan, The Beatles). Balanced treatments examine how the festival influenced an evolving popular music culture both as a commodity and as an art form (Hillstrom and Hillstrom, 2013).

Interestingly, the iconic nature and cultural importance of the Woodstock Music and Art Fair was not initially realized, emphasized, or reported by major news media. One study examined six daily newspapers (*New York Times, Washington Post, Wall Street Journal, Chicago Tribune, Los Angeles Times,* and *Cincinnati Enquirer*) and three magazines (*Time, Life,* and *Rolling Stone*) through the lens of framing theory to determine the prominence of the news event, the sources of information used to compile the coverage, and the extent to which the cultural aspects were given attention. The findings indicate each publication used primarily official sources such as law enforcement representatives, as opposed to consulting actual attendees. As a result, the coverage focused mainly on the problems created by the festival rather than the broader social implications and overarching significances (Sheehy, 2012). Initial postmortem analysis focused on then contemporary youth as a positive social force evidenced by the relative peacefulness of the festival or as the noble savage (Denisoff, 1986).

Ultimately, the Woodstock Music and Art Fair is a meaningful event, if nothing more, in the personal histories of baby boomers with many reflecting on the utopian symbolism and few on the music itself (Street, 2012). Personal histories reveal boomers who "seem to date their life using the festival as a major milestone" (Makower, 2009). The idealism of a generation is manifested symbolically in the phenomenon of Woodstock. The strong antiwar movement created a desire among many young people to reject the representations of the military-industrial complex and the associated political infrastructure. This led to an increased interest in "establishing self-sufficient communes" (Perone, 2005). Woodstock was the brief manifestation of this idealism, whether accurately or not, on such a large-scale as not to be soon forgotten.

The festival was, and continues to be, experienced by both attendees and non-attendees due to mass media and the subsequent film and sound recordings. The impact continues through all the subsequent years, from serving as a short-handed description of an entire youth movement to the anniversary concerts and their own attendant issues. This collection of all relevant research and essays, as well as significant primary and secondary sources, should serve well students, scholars, researchers, and news outlets. The contents will facilitate teaching, learning, and research. Vetted for relevance and accompanied by detailed informative annotations, this resource directs readers to notable scholarship on an "intense, extensive, and transitory" *gemeinschaft-gesellschaft* (Fine, 2012).

Photo by Mark Goff, image in the public domain. Wikimedia, https://commons.
wikimedia.org/wiki/File:Swami_opening.jpg

Culture & Society

Books

1. Arrigo, Bruce A., Dragan Milovanovic, and Robert Carl Schehr. *The French Connection in Criminology: Rediscovering Crime, Law, and Social Change.* Albany, NY: State University of New York Press, 2005.

Explores the sociology of crime. Describes the systems theory of "self-similarity" in which "behavior never repeats itself because it does not precisely follow the same path twice." Claims attempts to replicate events never completely duplicate the original because "there is always a degree of sensitivity to the initial conditions that established the behavior in the first place." Offers the attempts to replicate the social and cultural experiences of the 1969 Woodstock Music and Art Fair through Woodstock '94 and Woodstock '99 are examples of problems associated with iteration and self-similarity. Notes failure occurred in these instances even after attempts to invoke the same conditions of location, time of year, etc.

2. Bennett, Andy, ed. *Remembering Woodstock.* Aldershot, U.K.: Ashgate, 2004.

Collects nine essays examining the mythological and iconic status of the Woodstock Music and Art Fair as well as using the event as a starting point for broader analyses of popular culture, music, and nostalgia. Looks both forwards and backwards from the festival with sociological, historical, and musicological perspectives. Provides contexts for appreciating the event's "socio-cultural significance." Examines multiple topics, including Woodstock's influence on the music industry and its role regarding the power of music to influence political activities. Includes an introductory essay by the editor providing a sense of the various social and political streams (e.g., Vietnam War, Civil Rights Movement) collectively symbolized in cultural history by the Woodstock festival.

     http://dx.doi.org/10.11647/OBP.0105.01

3.   Brokaw, Tom. *Boom! Voices of the Sixties*. New York: Random House, 2007.

> Focuses on individuals who helped shape or were shaped by the political and cultural nature of the 1960s. Comments briefly on the experience of Tim Russert, Washington D.C. bureau chief for NBC News and host of the television show *Meet the Press*, attending the Woodstock Music and Art Fair with his three buddies and eight cases of beer. Relates a rumor heard by Russert alleging Johnny Carson was going to make an appearance at the festival. Includes a timeline of key events from the decade.

4.   Casale, Anthony M., and Philip Lerman. *Where have all the Flowers Gone?: The Fall and Rise of the Woodstock Generation*. Kansas City, MO: Andrews and McMeel, 1989.

> Explores baby boomers and the idealism of their generation as manifested symbolically at the Woodstock Music and Art Fair. Suggests that, after two decades of having been submerged, the ethos will resurface in the 1990s. Explains how the idealism was born out of the nation's effort to accommodate the sudden population growth created by the baby boomers. Focuses on Abbie Hoffman's involvement with the planning process for Woodstock and his activities on and off stage during the concert. Provides numerous stories of individuals and how they experienced the festival as both attendees and non-attendees. Delves into Michael Lang's involvement, or lack thereof, in several attempts to re-create Woodstock through tenth and twenty anniversary events.

5.   Curry, Jack. *Woodstock: The Summer of our Lives*. New York: Weidenfeld & Nicolson, 1989.

> Provides a qualitative look at the Woodstock Music and Art Fair in response to what the author claims are decades of writings emphasizing "sociology, crowd psychology, the weekend's cultural relevance" and perhaps irrelevance. Attempts to recapture the personal stories lost to the many mass movement analyses that typically consider the individuals at the festival as only particles in a larger social structure. Acknowledges time has affected the accuracy of some recollections, but characterizes this as reflecting the looseness and fluidity of the event itself. Emphasizes the unique emotional impact of the concert on individuals, rather than serving to document the event for the historical record. Asserts that for attendees, Woodstock "created memories that still hold a primary place in their personal autobiographies." Begins and ends with Penny Stallings, a Woodstock Ventures employee, and includes numerous individuals in between, such as Country Joe McDonald, John Sebastian, and less well known individuals. Includes some photographs from the festival.

6.   Denisoff, R. Serge. *Tarnished Gold: The Record Industry Revisited.* New Brunswick, NJ: Transaction Books, 1986.

> Touches on the politicization of rock music and the demise of rock music culture. Claims the importance of the Woodstock Music and Art Fair cannot be overstated. Notes the festival "generated an ethos, a mythology." Reports the dire conditions at the festival created a *"gemeinschaft* or communal aspect of the gathering." Observes "Woodstock transcended the most far-fetched dreams of nineteenth-century utopian-anarchist writers," but suggests this image was perhaps mostly a media contrivance. Quotes several publications, such as *Rolling Stone* magazine (available at http://www.rollingstone.com/music/features/it-was-like-balling-for-the-first-time-19690920), to illustrate the hyperbole in the immediate aftermath of the event. Continues by contrasting Woodstock with the infamous Altamont Speedway concert held several months later, citing the latter as "the nail in the coffin of the rock culture of the sixties."

7.   Echols, Alice. *Shaky Ground: The '60s and its Aftershocks.* New York: Columbia University Press, 2002.

> Articulates pithily a significant impact of the Woodstock Music and Art Fair; the discovery by both managers and musicians of the commercial benefits behind playing one large concert as opposed to many smaller ones. Notes one result was the beginning of the end to many "hippie ballrooms" of the era, such as the Avalon Ballroom, the Fillmore, and the Fillmore East.

8.   Eliot, Marc. *Rockonomics: The Money Behind the Music.* New York: Franklin Watts, 1989.

> Provides insight on rock music as a commodity. Discusses the full history of the production, marketing, and consumption of rock music. Offers the Woodstock Music and Art Fair as a symbol of "the selling of progressive idealism for corporate profit." Relates how Albert Grossman, manager of notable popular performing artists, went to the festival to ensure his clients were paid and discovered John Roberts, one of the promoters, knew even then the event would not be the financial disaster it appeared. Notes "although the financial mismanagement of the festival wound up in several court cases," the motion picture *Woodstock* went on to gross more than $50 million. Suggests the reason the "magic" of the original Woodstock festival has not been repeated is because of economics, noting the fees charged by performers increased substantially as a result of Woodstock.

9.   Ennis, Philip H. *The Seventh Stream: The Emergence of Rocknroll in American Popular Music*. Hanover, NH: Wesleyan University Press (University Press of New England), 1992.

Studies the confluence of art, commerce, and politics. Notes the success of Country Joe and the Fish and other San Francisco bands of the 1960s when performing at large outdoor rock music festivals. Claims this feat was due to their experiences at numerous earlier Golden Gate park concerts. Contends the Woodstock Music and Art Fair was a "startling and energizing affirmation of rock culture." Offers the festival represented a break within the youth culture between the political and the apolitical. States Jimi Hendrix's rendition of *The Star Spangled Banner* was implicitly a collective "assertion of opposition to the war in Vietnam." Concludes the Altamont Speedway concert killed any counterculture momentum emanating from Woodstock.

10.   Fine, Gary Alan. *Tiny Publics: A Theory of Group Action and Culture*. New York: Russell Sage Foundation, 2012.

Demonstrates the connection between small group cultural and large-scale civic engagement. Argues the building blocks of society are born in small group behavior in which meaning is created and beliefs shared. Offers the Woodstock Music and Art Fair as an example of a "macrogathering" in which community is "intense, extensive, and transitory." Claims the festival was able to create an active identity recognized beyond the confines of the group. Notes how once a communal identity is created, it can shape society if "linked to causes and beliefs." Suggests Woodstock and other rock music festivals, such as Burning Man, represent groups with a desire to "control their own spaces" with the ability to establish "authority to set the rules for action in the face of external control." Acknowledges in these instances "identity is salient within the framework of the gathering, but its impact swiftly dissipates." States the challenge rests with keeping the identification created during the event from becoming just a nostalgic latency.

11.   Gair, Christopher. *The American Counterculture*. Edinburgh, Scotland: Edinburgh University Press, 2007.

Investigates the relationship between the counterculture and American popular culture. Looks at the appropriation of counterculture ethos by the film and record industries. Offers an interdisciplinary account of the economic and social reasons leading to an emergence of the counterculture. Discusses the motion picture *Woodstock* more than the event itself, noting the movie is "constructed to represent a particular version of events that offers a summary of many of the central tenets of countercultural identity in the late 1960s, and the selection of musicians that it includes contributes to the narrative structure, rather than merely accompanying it." Claims that the Altamont Speedway concert is often used to establish "a bipolar opposition to Woodstock" but this is "reductive and misleading." Uses scenes from the *Woodstock* film to demonstrate the illusion of the counterculture "offering genuine alternatives to dominant American life-styles." Devotes text to an interpretation of Jimi Hendrix's performance at the festival, concluding his "emergent racial consciousness exposes tensions at the heart of countercultural practice."

12. Goffman, Ken, and Dan Joy. *Counterculture through the Ages: From Abraham to Acid House.* New York: Villard, 2004.

Provides a history on the concept and manifestation of countercultures. Uses in passing the Woodstock Music and Art Fair to highlight the contradictory values held among the self-proclaimed members of the 1960s youth movement, especially between the commercialism of the rock music industry and the rank-and-file societal dropouts. Quotes Andy Warhol's comment on the audience at Woodstock. Foreword by Timothy Leary.

13. Grossman, Lloyd. *A Social History of Rock Music: From the Greasers to Glitter Rock.* New York: David McKay, 1976.

Invokes the Woodstock Music and Art Fair as an example of counterculture idealism quickly tainted after-the-fact by the commercialization of the Woodstock "product."

14. Hamelman, Steven L. *But is it Garbage?: On Rock and Trash.* Athens, GA: University of Georgia Press, 2004.

Claims "American culture is trash culture." Observes trash, both literal and figurative, as a catalyst for the transformation of musicians, critics, and consumers. Refers to both the 1969 Woodstock Music and Art Fair and Woodstock '99 as examples of producing garbage that is a by-product of large-scale rock music events. Notes the 1969 festival displayed a care-free and playful attitude toward the waste produced, using it to create "peace" messages without regard for its ultimate destiny. Points to Woodstock '99 where massive amounts of trash and unsanitary conditions became newsworthy. Speculates that "perhaps the deluge of waste complemented the sound of a civilization going into the dumpster." States both concerts teach us that garbage produced at these types of events is "staggering" in its volume and "live rock 'n' roll and trash are symbiotic."

15.	Harrington, Joe S. *Sonic Cool: The Life & Death of Rock 'n' Roll*. New York: Hal Leonard, 2002.

> Asserts rock music culture no longer exists as a socio-political entity. States the Woodstock Music and Art Fair presented contradictions for the revolutionary aspects of the 1960s youth movement. Notes the commercialism behind the staging of the event, the use of "machines manufactured by General Motors" to bring 500,000 people together, and the acceptance of food handouts from "the opposing forces" (i.e., the establishment).

16.	Henderson, Simon. *Sidelined: How American Sports Challenged the Black Freedom Struggle*. Lexington, KY: University Press of Kentucky, 2013. https://doi.org/10.5810/kentucky/9780813141541.001.0001

> Explores the ways in which African-American athletes utilized college and professional sports during the 1960s to communicate the struggle for civil rights. Focuses on the 1968 Olympics held in Mexico City where Tommie Smith and John Carlos protested by raising their fists on the podium after receiving their Olympic medals. Mentions several uses of *The Star Spangled Banner* to invoke controversy and make political statements. Asserts Jimi Hendrix's performance of the national anthem at the Woodstock Music and Art Fair was "largely regarded as a reflection of the loss of faith in American ideals and a call for redemption amid the turmoil of the Vietnam era."

17.	Hoffman, Abbie. *Woodstock Nation: A Talk-Rock Album*. New York: Vintage Books, 1969.

> Provides a first-person account from one of the vanguard leaders of the 1960s counterculture political front. Uses the Woodstock Music and Art Fair as the cornerstone event in a tour de force conceptualization of the "Woodstock Nation." Postulates on the relationship between rock music and politics. Dedicated to Lenny Bruce.

18.	Issitt, Micah L. *Hippies: A Guide to an American Subculture*. Santa Barbara, CA: Greenwood Press, 2009.

> Attempts to provide an informed view of a hippie, beyond the general notion of "a cultural rebel who advocates liberalism in both politics and lifestyle." Uses occasional mentions of the Woodstock Music and Art Fair as a cultural reference point. Asserts that the widely repeated belief that two babies were born at the festival has not been proven. Includes a timeline, biographical sketches, and an annotated bibliography.

19. Jacobs, Ron. *The Way the Wind Blew: A History of the Weather Underground*. London: Verso, 1997. https://libcom.org/files/32709343-Way-the-Wind-Blew-A-History-Of-The-Weather-Underground.pdf

Notes the Woodstock Music and Art Fair signaled to the rest of the world just how widespread the counterculture ethos had become, forcing political attention on this demographic. Includes a list of acronyms associated with the Weathermen, a chronology of significant events, and short biographies of key individuals.

20. Johnson, Bruce, and Martin Cloonan. *Dark Side of the Tune: Popular Music and Violence*. Burlington, VT: Ashgate, 2009.

Argues music, a fundamentally sonic phenomenon, has a relationship to violence. Examines the transformation of this relationship as caused by the introduction of technology. Offers the "most pervasive function of music in generating violence appears to be in everyday life" (as opposed to state-sponsored). Uses the riots at Woodstock '99 as an example of a mob seeking revenge for being denied what they perceived as entitlements. Recounts specific events from the concert, beginning with the group Limp Bizkit working the crowd into a frenzy and cumulating through the full-scale rioting. Details the lack of sanitation and water, excessive use of drug and alcohol, and capitalistic opportunism. Claims the mythology of the original Woodstock Music and Art Fair was an impossible and unreal standard to replicate at Woodstock '99. Notes music often offers to emancipate but its failure to do so creates a "point of angry focus" to "the accumulated force of all those other promises that consumerism fails to deliver." Concludes capitalism impinges on musical performance.

21. Jones, Landon Y. *Great Expectations: America and the Baby Boom Generation*. New York: Coward, McCann & Geoghegan, 1980.

Considers the impact of baby boomers over the decades, starting with early expectations of them becoming the best educated generation in history, born in an environment of continuous economic growth. Traces their influences: first creating a youth-centered culture, then becoming a political force based on idealism, and finally producing societal concerns regarding housing, medical care, and Social Security. Describes baby boomers as a "generational tyranny" because of the exceptional size of this particular demographic and its resulting impacts, both positive and negative, on a society that has no choice but to address. While discussion of the Woodstock Music and Art Fair is limited, this book does place the festival within the context of larger social issues surrounding baby boomers. Woodstock is characterized as being the cumulating event of all the major experiences uniquely defining the baby boom generation's evolution to that point.

22.   Klein, Naomi. *No Logo*. New York: Picador, 2002.

Articulates the cultural and economic conditions that create oppositional forces to the corporate takeover of society. Highlights in brief Woodstock '94 and the associated news media coverage while lamenting the overtly commercialization of the Woodstock ethos. Notes "the debate revolved around the sanctity of the past, with no recognition of present-tense cultural challenges." Observes news media focused on the significance of Woodstock '94 to aging baby boomers instead of on members of the youth market for which the event was organized. States there was no exploration of the meaning commodification created for today's youth. Offers those attending Woodstock '94 had their generational identity prepackaged and marketed long before arriving at the concert.

23.   Mercer, Kobena. *Welcome to the Jungle: New Positions in Black Cultural Studies*. New York: Routledge, 1994.

Invokes very succinctly the Woodstock Music and Art Fair to illustrate the concept of an "ambiguous appropriation of black expressive culture." Suggests the festival exemplifies the notion of an "imagined community," in this case one of white middle-class youth separate from society (i.e., Woodstock nation). States Jimi Hendrix's deconstruction of *The Star Spangled Banner* questioned the validity of the imagined community's "conditions of representability."

24.   Miles, Barry. *Hippie*. New York: Sterling, 2004.

Presents an illustrated and exhaustive commentary on the counterculture movement of the 1960s. Places numerous milestone events in political, historical, and cultural contexts. Dedicates some text to the 1969 Woodstock Music and Art Fair, the subsequent film, and related anniversary events.

25.   Miller, Timothy. *The Hippies and American Values*. Knoxville, TN: University of Tennessee Press, 2011.

Explains how the Woodstock Music and Art Fair was, despite initial unfavorable press, "quickly mythologized by the counterculture as the epitome of joy and peace." Offers the festival's meaning to the counterculture was as "a cataclysm, a political event, a religious experience, a glimpse of communal solidarity, the pinnacle of passive consumerism, and the first free dope territory in America." Claims

Woodstock and other rock music festivals of the same time period created a tremendous sense of community and a desire for ongoing communal experiences that could be created almost spontaneously. Asserts counterculture membership came to be defined by self-sacrifice for the greater communal good. Connects the festival to the then growing counterculture desire to be free from the concept of money being a necessity for life. Also connects Woodstock with a confirmation among members of the counterculture that a drug revolution favoring greater freedoms was in full strength.

26.   Pell, George, Cardinal. *God and Caesar: Selected Essays on Religion, Politics, & Society.* Ed. M. A. Casey. Washington, D.C.: Catholic University of America Press, 2011.

Draws upon the author's essays concerning key issues for Christians in "determining the future of modern democratic life." Contends Woodstock '99, with its rioting, arson, and rapes, was an inevitable progression from the 1969 Woodstock Music and Art Fair. Notes participants at both festivals were rejecting their parent's values, thus Woodstock '99 was the act of 1960s pacifism being spurned. Suggests the Woodstock concept of liberty only traps people into a chaos derived from suppressed emotions with negative consequences.

27.   Pettman, Dominic. *After the Orgy: Toward a Politics of Exhaustion.* Albany, NY: State University of New York Press, 2002.

Ponders the Dionysian cult of the 1960s as manifested in the sexual revolution and the possible underlying cause of its social acceptability (i.e., a "profound fear of apocalypse" caused by an atomic bomb-inspired cold war and the Vietnam War). Offers how the often used symbolism attributed to the Woodstock Music and Art Fair of representing a 1960s degenerating utopia fails to "take into account the horror and panic that encouraged the 'free love' in the first place."

28.   Powers, Devon. *Writing the Record: The Village Voice and the Birth of Rock Criticism.* Amherst, MA: University of Massachusetts Press, 2013.

Presents a history of key rock music critics and their legacy. Highlights an analysis of Craig Karpel's critique of "hip capitalist" in the music business who tried to profit from the anti-capitalistic values of the counterculture. Offers the Woodstock Music and Art Fair as the "best example of the mutable relationship among capitalism, music, and the counterculture." Asks why the event is considered a triumph over capitalism when, in fact, it was a capitalistic undertaking from the very beginning. Explores whether an underlying ambivalence of the youth movement to consumerism allowed a co-opting of hippie ethos.

29. Pratt, Ray. *Rhythm and Resistance: Explorations of Political Uses of Popular Music.* New York: Praeger, 1990.

Interprets the political uses of popular music over the last two-hundred years of American history. Defines popular music as an attempt to create community in the face of social transformations. Refers to the Woodstock Music and Art Fair as being the apex of "explicitly political popular music." Notes the festival was a symbol of "oppositional popular culture" and fed into a fantasy of creating a new type of self-sufficient community based on the joy of music.

30. Rosenman, Joel, John Roberts, and Robert Pilpel. *Young Men with Unlimited Capital.* New York: Harcourt Brace Jovanovich, 1974.

Chronicles the business machinations leading up to the Woodstock Music and Art Fair. Provides narrative first-hand details on forming personal partnerships, dealing with the banks, attempting to secure a site, working with complicating zoning laws, handling building permits, managing third parties trying to get in on the action (or at least profit from it), and following the money (or at least trying to). Describes the first meeting of the four key promoters: Michael Lang, Artie Kornfeld, Joel Rosenman, and John Roberts. Narrates key meetings, such as with the Wallkill Zoning Board of Appeals, occurring along the way to solidifying the logistics for the festival. Introduces key personnel of Woodstock Ventures, the company formed to marshal resources for the event. Details how the festival site was eventually finalized on the farm of Max Yasgur. Mentions Abbie Hoffman attempting to extort money from the promoters. Relates how the Hog Farm commune came to be engaged "for peace-keeping, medical, and general assistance purposes." Conveys how a local performance by the Earthlite Theater in White Lake, New York, nearly derailed the festival because the actors stripped on stage. Offers day-to-day perspectives on the actual event from both Rosenman and Roberts. Explains the crisis created when the Grateful Dead's manager demanded payment upfront before his band would take the stage. Includes a somewhat humorous profit/loss statement as of December 31, 1973.

31. Rubin, Jerry. *Do it!: Scenarios of the Revolution.* New York: Simon and Schuster, 1970.

Represents a counterculture political manifesto, somewhat. Makes a passing reference to the Woodstock Music and Art Fair as a "spontaneous triumph of anarchy." Introduction to the book by Eldridge Cleaver.

32. Ruiz, Teofilo F. *The Terror of History: On the Uncertainties of Life in Western Civilization.* Princeton, NJ: Princeton University Press, 2011. https://doi.org/10.1515/9781400839421

Contemplates the "human response to the terror of history" and how humanity seeks to create meaning of the world and events. Considers the ways in which this is done, through embracing religious experiences to pursuing material wealth. Believes these are attempts at escapism. Mentions the Woodstock Music and Art Fair as an example of how many live vicariously through the actions of others (i.e., many claim to have attended the festival although they, in fact, did not). States the idealized combination of music, peace, and nonviolence provided a "slim possibility to dehistoricize our lives" and this is why the concept of Woodstock still resonates.

33. Smith, Chas. *From Woodstock to the Moon: The Cultural Evolution of Rock Music.* Dubuque, IA: Kendall/Hunt, 2001.

Serves as a middle-school textbook and is included here mostly as an artifact. Discusses the notion of tribalism that evolved in the 1960s among members of the counterculture. Offers the Woodstock Music and Art Fair as the cumulating tribal event. Claims the drenching rain storms provided a sought after "moment of pure egalitarianism."

34. Street, John. *Rebel Rock: The Politics of Popular Music.* Oxford: Basil Blackwell, 1986.

Explores the ways in which political bodies make use of popular music to pursue their agendas, the ways in which popular music is created and managed by the music industry, and how popular music acquires meaning through consumption. Describes the calculated methods used to exploit the counterculture ethos in producing the Woodstock Music and Art Fair. Compares and contrasts the 1969 festival with the Live Aid concert in the 1985.

35. Sylvan, Robin. *Traces of the Spirit: The Religious Dimensions of Popular Music.* New York: New York University Press, 2002.

Reports on continuity from religious revival camp meetings from the eighteenth and nineteenth centuries to the Woodstock Music and Art Fair in 1969. Suggests the festival and the ones following represented a larger religious transformation. Claims by the late 1960s, rock music had become an "important voice in the political and cultural changes" sweeping America. Notes that a cultural transformation, however, did not occur, despite Woodstock having demonstrated "the ability of the counterculture to create what seemed to many a workable alternative community on an unprecedented scale based on the values of peace and love" and founded on rock music.

36. Weiner, Rex, and Deanne Stillman. *Woodstock Census: The Nationwide Survey of the Sixties Generation.* New York: Viking Press, 1979. https://erowid.org/library/books_online/woodstock_census.pdf

Surveys self-selected members of the Woodstock generation regarding their experiences during the 1960s and the 1970s. Reports 17% of respondents consider the Woodstock Music and Art Fair to be "one of the best experiences of the era." Presents several comments on the festival, mostly positive, from respondents who reported attending the event. Includes a copy of the survey instrument and data results.

37. Werner, Craig. *A Change is Gonna Come: Music, Race & the Soul of America.* New York: Plume, 1999.

Explores relationships between popular music and racial politics. Comments briefly on the Woodstock Music and Art Fair in the context of rock music festivals of the 1960s and their overall lack of significance to the African-American community. Suggest even the black performers at Woodstock did not perform *soul* music. Focuses on Jimi Hendrix and Otis Redding as representatives of African-American music to white audiences.

38. Wiener, Jon. *Come Together: John Lennon in His Time.* New York: Random House, 1984.

Surveys the political life of John Lennon. Touches quickly on the role of rock music festivals as political expressions. Observes the Woodstock Music and Art Fair highlighted the extent to which the political radicals of the 1960s were weak within the overall counterculture movement. Relays a rejection by the promoters of Woodstock of an offer by John Lennon to play the festival after he said he could not deliver the Beatles.

39. Zolov, Eric. *Refried Elvis: The Rise of the Mexican Counterculture.* Berkeley, CA: University of California Press, 1999.

Shows the influence of rock music on Mexico's social, cultural, and political environments. Uses the 1968 student movement and the Mexican regime's "crisis of authority" as a point of reference. Discusses the 1971

Avandaro rock music festival that used the Woodstock Music and Art Fair as a model. Claims Avandaro "represented the appropriation of a vanguard image of modernity borrowed from Woodstock and fused with local cultural practice," but Woodstock itself borrowed and romanticized elements of Mexican folk culture. Explains how the Woodstock festival had become "a parable for the story of the United States itself." Notes Woodstock symbolized a productive relationship between public culture and private enterprise. Suggests the "urban middle-class youth around the world were eagerly appropriating the images, language, music" of Woodstock for their own purposes of rebellion. Observes unlike ongoing cultural influences of Woodstock, Avandaro's legacy has been "repressed in the name of cultural imperialism."

Chapters

40. Ambrose, Joe. "White Riot — Woodstock '99." *Moshpit: The Violent World of Mosh Pit Culture.* London: Omnibus Press, 2001. 15–26.

Asserts Woodstock '99 gave America "a wake-up call as stark as that which the original festival gave in '69." Notes the original Woodstock Music and Art Fair was about youth "making love" whereas Woodstock '99 was about youth "making war," referencing the violence associated with the latter. Reports on the "atmosphere of claustrophobic sexism" at Woodstock '99 and how it was exhibited to the world through televised pay-per-view. Describes the contexts which led to the rioting. Places some of the blame on the performance by the band Limp Bizkit during which singer Fred Durst incited violent behavior. Relays specific instances of rape in the mosh pit. Suggests some of the events at the earlier Woodstock '94 foreshadowed the Woodstock '99 disaster. Offers the Woodstock '99 rioters represented "middle-class white kids getting away with murder in situations where Black and Latino kids would have been crushed." Quotes some of the performers' observations about the violence.

41. Anderson, Terry H. "Counterculture." *The Movement and the Sixties.* New York: Oxford University Press, 1995. 241–291.

Attempts to define and explain the social activism of the 1960s. Examines the youth movement which evolved in response to the political and social environment of the cold war era. Describes membership in the counterculture as being an individualistic journey. Covers the Civil Rights Movement, the drug culture, and the Vietnam War. States the somewhat isolated rural setting of the Woodstock Music and Art Fair resulted in participants establishing "their own culture with their own rules, rituals, costumes, and standards of behavior." Observes the festival's various potential disasters associated with poor sanitation and lack of food generated a growing sense of community which, in turn, created an "an unforgettable countercultural experience." Explains how Woodstock as a phenomenon led underground cultural figures to view it as a beginning of a political youth movement. Continues by noting major concurrent events of 1969, the Manson murders and the disastrous Altamont Speedway concert, quickly sidetracked the utopianism created by Woodstock.

42. Baritz, Loren. "Culture War." *The Good Life: The Meaning of Success for the American Middle Class.* New York: Alfred A. Knopf, 1989. 225–288.

Articulates the potential power of the 1960s youth movement and uses concisely the Woodstock Music and Art Fair to illustrate. Claims many individuals assumed the festival unleashed generational pressures that "would finally free America." Concludes the cultural upheaval was based on "the force of irrationality."

43. "Between Paradise and Apocalypse." *Interviews with Northrop Frye.* Ed. Jean O'Grady. v. 24. Toronto, Canada: University of Toronto Press, 2008. 367–399. https://doi.org/10.3138/9781442688377-043

Transcribes an interview with literary critic Northrop Frye conducted in February 1978 by Don Harron. Converses on a diverse religious awakening emergent from the 1960s counterculture. Comments on the Woodstock Music and Art Fair in a comparison of religious revivals with political rallies. Frye offers "Woodstock was the most obviously Dionysiac phenomenon that there's been in modern society." States that the festival was "a rather pathetic illusion that somehow or other you could, again, break through the crust of history and get into a different way of existence altogether by a kind of emotional release."

44. Bloustien, Gerry. "Still Picking Children from the Trees? Reimagining Woodstock in Twenty-First-Century Australia." *Remembering Woodstock.* Ed. Andy Bennett. Aldershot, U.K.: Ashgate, 2004. 127–145.

Demonstrates how the legacy of the Woodstock Music and Art Fair "still reverberates in time and space, far from its original source." Uses WOMAD (World of Music, Arts and Dance) as an example of a manifestation of nostalgia for a "return to the Woodstock dream, if not the reality." Contends a desire for shared experience is fulfilled through the dramatization of myth (i.e., re-enacting the spirit of Woodstock).

45. Brackett, David. "Festivals: The Good, the Bad, and the Ugly." *The Pop, Rock, and Soul Reader: Histories and Debates.* New York: Oxford University Press, 2005. 223–229.

Devotes an essay to rock music festivals. Comments on J. R. Young's "review" of the album *Woodstock: Music from the Original Soundtrack and More* appearing originally in *Rolling Stone* magazine (July 9, 1970). Notes the review highlights self-delusion within the counterculture of the 1960s. Incorporates a reprint of the review. Includes a section on the infamous Altamont Speedway concert featuring the Rolling Stones.

46. Chapple, Steve, and Rebee Garofalo. "The Expanded Industry." *Rock 'n' Roll is here to Pay: The History and Politics of the Music Industry.* Chicago: Nelson Hall, 1977. 123–169.

Begins with the premise of rock music being the "the most important cultural expression in the United States today." Covers the topics of agents, managers, and promoters before launching into a discussion on the staging of rock concerts. Mentions the value of the Monterey International Pop Festival in bringing to the attention of record companies many up and coming rock acts. Focuses on the financial mess created by the disorganization of the Woodstock Music and Art Fair. Notes the relatively young age of the festival's promoters. Highlights in what ways the event was a good example of the counterculture profiting off of the counterculture. Explains the actual profits came from the subsequent Woodstock film and sound recordings. Suggests Woodstock attendees were merely "the largest unpaid studio audience in history." Continues with a discussion of the Altamont Speedway concert. Concludes with a commentary on the rock music press and its relationship with, and role within, the rest of the industry.

47. Dessner, Lawrence J. "Woodstock: A Nation at War." *Things in the Driver's Seat: Readings in Popular Culture.* Ed. Harry Russell Huebel. Chicago: Rand McNally, 1972. 245–251.

Suggests participants in the Woodstock Music and Art Fair represent a coming together of a new community, later reproduced and enlarged through the motion picture *Woodstock*. Offers this new community has repudiated violence by virtue of their expressed moral opposition the Vietnam War, yet has reproduced itself in the "mirror images of the very war they oppose." Supports this assertion by noting approximately the same number of persons attending the festival, an invading force into rural America, equaled the number of Americans who went to Vietnam. Notes the natives of Bethel, New York, supplied basic necessities but did not engage with the "invaders." Continues by drawing numerous parallels between the invading American military and the invading Woodstock audience and promoters, including the eventual abandoning of the scarred battlefield. Concludes Woodstock was a manifestation of "a paradigm of the military culture."

48.   Diltz, Henry. "Jimi Hendrix Playing at Woodstock." *Government, Politics, and Protest: Essential Primary Sources.* Eds. K. Lee Lerner, Brenda Wilmoth Lerner, and Adrienne Wilmoth Lerner. Detroit, MI: Thomson, 2006. 20–22.

Focuses on the significance of Jimi Hendrix's performance at the Woodstock Music and Art Fair. Notes how Hendrix did not get to perform until Monday morning, thus the audience was lethargic due to three days of exhaustion. Adds his band was poorly rehearsed. Considers it to be, in the end, "one of history's most important rock performances." Summarizes the 1969 festival's place in contemporary culture.

49.   Dotter, Daniel. "Rock and Roll is here to Stray: Youth Subculture, Deviance, and Social Typing in Rock's Early Years." *Adolescents and their Music: If it's Too Loud, You're Too Old.* Ed. Jonathan S. Epstein. New York: Garland, 1994. 87–114.

Studies the relationship between rock music and deviant behavior in the early years (1950s) of the genre. Looks at the facilitating role of mass media and the social construction of deviance. Contrasts with the evolution to the 1960s when lifestyle deviance married with political deviance. Discusses the Woodstock Music and Art Fair as being the zenith of such deviance. Suggests the festival was both "a celebration of and also an obituary for the 1960s." Continues by noting the further evolution of these two types of deviance (lifestyle and political) into commercial commodities through positive presentation in the media.

50.   Fischer, Klaus P. "Countercultural Protest Movements." *America in White, Black, and Gray: The Stormy 1960s.* New York: Continuum International, 2006. 295–335.

Questions whether the youth movement of the 1960s represented a true counterculture. Focuses on the rise of the hippie culture as a reaction to the previous generation's middle-class conventions and the demands for a more inclusive and liberal society. Includes a section on "The Myth of the Woodstock Nation." Claims the Woodstock Music and Art Fair "gave the world a visual sense of the new lifestyle in action." Describes the new lifestyle as primitive tribal bonding with Woodstock being a metaphor for a state of mind. States both positive and negative views of the festival are overblown, noting the event did not, in fact, signal a cultural paradigm shift in any direction. Acknowledges Woodstock was a heightened "split between Dionysian protest and a decaying form of Apollonian mainstream." Argues the counterculture rebellion against capitalism, in the end, strengthened the economic model.

51. Glausser, Wayne. "Santana." *Cultural Encyclopedia of LSD*. Jefferson, NC: McFarland, 2011. 141.

States the defining moment for the music group Santana was their performance at the Woodstock Music and Art Fair. Reports Carlos Santana later admitting to being under the influence of LSD during their set, claiming it was "beyond scary."

52. Gordon, Andy. "Satan & the Angels: Paradise Loused." *Altamont: Death of Innocence in the Woodstock Nation*. Ed. Jonathan Eisen. New York: Avon Books, 1970. 30–71.

Traces the lead up to the Altamont Speedway concert through a discussion grounded in the traditions of the harvest festival and the town jester ("sanctioned release for anarchic and satanic impulse"). Starts with the 1964 Newport Folk Festival, then moves through the mid-1960s San Francisco scene and the 1968 Chicago riots, to 1969's Woodstock Music and Art Fair and then to Altamont Speedway. Likens the Woodstock myth to *Huckleberry Finn* contrasted with Altamont Speedway being like *Lord of the Flies*. The remainder of the book is built around this chapter.

53. Klein, Pip. "A Woodstock Festivalgoer Explains Why the Experience Cannot be Reproduced." *Perspectives on Modern World History: Woodstock*. Ed. Louise I. Gerdes. Detroit, MI: Greenhaven Press, 2012. 199–203.

Recounts the author's attendance in 1998 at a Woodstock commemorative concert held at Monticello Raceway near the site of the 1969 Woodstock Music and Art Fair. Articulates the differences between the two events, including the ease of parking, selling of expensive t-shirts, and presence of ATMs. Describes attending the 1969 festival as an "eclipse" because one was "there watching it, you know that it's an incredible coming together of cosmic forces — and it's never going to happen again." Notes the nostalgia value of attending these more recent happenings because "you can dream, even if you can't go home again." Includes a humorous chart contrasting the 1969 and 1998 events.

54. Kopkind, Andrew. "Coming of Age in Aquarius." *Takin' it to the Streets: A Sixties Reader.* Eds. Alexander Bloom and Wini Breines. New York: Oxford University Press, 2003. 511–516.

> Presents a politicized account of the Woodstock Music and Art Fair. Compares it to the French revolution and the San Francisco earthquake. Claims the festival "defied categories and conventional perceptions." Focuses on the cooptation and commercialization of the counterculture ethos, suggesting the event was "a test of the ability of avant-garde capitalism at once to profit from and control the insurgencies which its system spawns." Declares the event to represent a new culture of opposition.

55. Laing, Dave. "The Three Woodstocks and the Live Music Scene." *Remembering Woodstock.* Ed. Andy Bennett. Aldershot, U.K.: Ashgate, 2004. 1–17.

> Uses the three Woodstock concerts (1969, 1994, and 1999) as well as other major rock music festivals to illustrate an increasingly corporatization of live music presentations. Compares and contrasts the three events. Focuses on three elements: a) the evolution of music festivals as carnival, where the attraction is to be part of an event as opposed to seeing and hearing any one particular performer, b) the evolution of the music festival business from entrepreneurial to corporate enterprise, and c) the "deterritorialization" of live music events due to increased access via technology. Views the original 1969 Woodstock festival as the "fatal moment" when idealism and commercialism became disentwined.

56. Lieberman, Paul. "Some Festivalgoers Continue to Promote the Ideal of the Woodstock Generation." *Perspectives on Modern World History: Woodstock.* Ed. Louise I. Gerdes. Detroit, MI: Greenhaven Press, 2012. 111–121.

> Reprints an August 15, 2009, article from the *Los Angeles Times* in which the author admits to using government anti-poverty funds to purchase a bus in order to haul himself and his frustrated social-activists associates "over the Berkshires" to the Woodstock Music and Art Fair in the summer of 1969. Profiles his comrades and details the circumstances leading to the adventure. Relates their experience at the concert. Provides an update on each participant and describes how they continue to address social issues. Includes a sidebar on Wavy Gravy.

57. Lytle, Mark Hamilton. "The Uncivil Wars: Woodstock to Kent State." *America's Uncivil Wars: The Sixties Era from Elvis to the Fall of Richard Nixon.* New York: Oxford University Press, 2006. 334–356.

Suggests the positive outcome of the Woodstock Music and Art Fair was it being viewed as a "revolution in consciousness," referencing Charles Reich's bestseller *The Greening of America.* Then claims this was a naïve perspective because the festival was a unique occurrence due to a confluence of circumstance and any attempts to repeat it would likely be corrupted by commercialism. Offers the Altamont Speedway concert as evidence. Comments on the symbolic links that have been made between the Manson murders and Altamont. Claims commercialism is the "most defining quality of American culture." Asserts the deteriorating drug culture and associated violence helped destroy the counterculture. Continues with an analysis of Richard Nixon's politics, his presidency, the Vietnam War opposition, and how this political unrest climaxed symbolically with the Kent State shootings.

58. Meade, Marion. "The Degradation of Women." *The Sounds of Social Change.* Eds. R. Serge Denisoff and Richard A. Peterson. Chicago: Rand McNally, 1972. 173–177.

Starts with conveying the author's reaction to the motion picture *Woodstock.* States she found the film disturbing because all the performers shown, except for Joan Baez, were men. Notes men are depicted in the movie "building the stage, directing traffic, shooting the film, and running the festival." Offers women are portrayed cooking, feeding babies, or "sprawled erotically in the grass." Uses the film to confirm the notion of rock music culture being degrading to women.

59. Moore, Allan F. "The Contradictory Aesthetics of Woodstock." *Remembering Woodstock.* Ed. Andy Bennett. Aldershot, U.K.: Ashgate, 2004. 75–89.

Theorizes the phrase "Woodstock Nation" implies a relationship between music and society that may be, in fact, illusionary — that "certain musical practices acted as a universalizing social force." Seeks to connect the attributions of a "Woodstock Nation" to selected musical performances at the Woodstock Music and Art Fair. Itemizes the varied musical styles represented at the festival as: acoustic singer, retro rock and roll, progressive blues, blue-eyed soul, psychedelia, country rock, soul funk, straight-ahead rock, and unrestrainedly exotic (Ravi

Shankar). Concludes contradictory performances "both in terms of stylistic parameters and in terms of their expression of social values" did reflect the counterculture and a conflict inherent in maintaining both individuality and social structure.

60. Mottram, Eric. "Dionysus in America." *Blood on the Nash Ambassador: Investigations in American Culture.* London: Hutchinson Radius, 1989. 181–220.

Collects essays written by the author representing studies on American culture. Traces the experimental art forms emerging in the 1950s and 1960s to America's nineteenth-century past. Describes rock music as a specifically American art with social and political implications challenging traditional forms. Explores the impact of electronically produced music on the emergence of rock music. Focuses on the music group The Doors as representing an expression of the Dionysus experience. Offers the Woodstock Music and Art Fair and the Altamont Speedway concert as "Dionysian energy polarized finally between two distinct events." Discusses the Dionysian context of Woodstock. Follows by contrasting the ethos of Altamont Speedway concert's "working class" audience with Woodstock's "middle class" attendees as a possible explanation for the very different experiences.

61. Myers, Alice. "Woodstock Concerts." *The Nineties in America.* Ed. Milton Berman. v. 3. Pasadena, CA: Salem Press, 2009. 933–935.

Contrast both Woodstock '94 and Woodstock '99 with the original 1969 Woodstock Music and Art Fair. Notes Woodstock '94 was markedly different due to the presence of heavy corporate sponsorship and overt commercialism. Observes Woodstock '99 was marred by violence due to a shift in social norms among the youth culture. Comments the 1999 concert also introduced use of the Internet as a promotional means. Claims the significance of the two events in the 1990s was the "the appropriation of counterculture by marketing" and the evolution of rock festivals into "global media events."

62. Rand, Ayn. "Apollo and Dionysus." *The New Left: The Anti-Industrial Revolution.* New York: New American Library, 1970. 57–81. https://campus.aynrand.org/works/1969/01/01/apollo-and-dionysus

Contains Rand's treatise on Apollo and Dionysus in which she evokes the Apollo moon landing and the Woodstock Music and Art Fair to illustrate reason versus emotions. Delves into how the news media portrayed and discussed both events. Offers the moon landing as an example the highest of ideals and Woodstock as the lowest. Claims these two events from 1969 demonstrate "specific forms in which philosophical abstractions appear in our actual existence."

63. Rectanus, Mark W. "Sponsoring Events: Culture as Corporate Stage, From Woodstock to Ravestock and Reichstock." *Culture Incorporated: Museums, Artists, and Corporate Sponsorship.* Minneapolis, MN: University of Minnesota Press, 2002. 132–168.

Examines the relationships of corporations, art institutions, and foundations and the effects on culture. Explores corporate sponsored cultural events and associated implications. Holds the Woodstock Music and Art Fair as one of two examples of unsponsored events "represented in the media as expressions of resistance to or subversion of commodified culture." Acknowledges Woodstock was not intended to be a rejection of commodified culture, it was, rather, a failed commercial venture. Explains how a sense of community arose spontaneously as a reaction to the unexpected magnitude of the festival combined with the adverse weather conditions. Points to Woodstock '94 and Woodstock '99 as demonstrating how "institutionalized production and signification of the event by the media and sponsors assumes a pivotal position." Notes the original 1969 Woodstock festival had to be deconstructed and reconfigured in order to market Woodstock '94 in terms of serving "apolitical, environmentally friendly, and technological conscious consumerism." Describes Woodstock '99 as the opposite of the 1969 concert in terms of greed and violence, noting the primary objective of the former was purely profit motivated. The second example highlighted in this chapter is the art piece *Wrapped Reichstag* by artists Christo and Jeanne-Claude. Suggests both Woodstock and *Wrapped Reichstag* accumulated cultural capital by signifying a political ethos.

64. Rodrick, Stephen. "The Woodstock 1994 Festival Reflects Cultural Changes." *Perspectives on Modern World History: Woodstock.* Ed. Louise I. Gerdes. Detroit, MI: Greenhaven Press, 2012. 171–175.

Reprints an article first appearing in *The New Republic* (September 5, 1994). Discusses marketing excesses of Woodstock '94 and the aggressive audience backlash. Describes violence in the mosh pit as "terrorism." Contrasts with the peacefulness of attendees at the original 1969 Woodstock Music and Art Fair.

65. Schuman, Howard, Robert F. Belli, and Katherine Bischoping. "The Generational Basis of Historical Knowledge." *Collective Memory* *of Political Events: Social Psychological Perspectives.* Eds. James W. Pennebaker, Dario Paez, and Bernard Rime. Mahwah, NJ: Lawrence Erlbaum, 1997. 47–77. https://doi.org/10.4324/9780203774427

> Hypothesizes one is likely to have accurate knowledge of events occurring prior to birth and knowledge of past events declines gradually; adolescence provides a unique time in one's life to acquire knowledge of large-scale events outside of one's own life and, therefore, adults who were older when an event occurs will have less knowledge of the event than adolescents; and gender and race affect knowledge of events when they have a personal meaning in relation to it. Includes the Woodstock Music and Art Fair as one of eleven events used to test the hypotheses. Notes that the Holocaust and Woodstock were described adequately by more than 60% of respondents, compared to less than 15% for the Marshall Plan. Notes the Woodstock results show "clear evidence of the predicted curvilinear relations to age." Suggests openness to new knowledge and the imprint of first experiences during adolescence accounts for the conclusion.

66.   Sobran, Joseph. "The Fans at Woodstock were Outcasts Looking for Belonging." *Perspectives on Modern World History: Woodstock.* Ed. Louise I. Gerdes. Detroit, MI: Greenhaven Press, 2012. 102–110.

> Asserts hippies, as represented by those attending the Woodstock Music and Art Fair in 1969, "were positively hungry for authority" and they settled for it in the only available form of peer pressure. Claims the stereotypical image of hippies was a realistic portrayal in that they all looked and talked alike. Insists Woodstock proved "when their numbers reach critical mass, they become a market, and you can herd them together and tell them things they desperately want to hear," such as how all their unresolved personal problems are really only one big political problem that can be solved instantaneously. Originally published in *National Review* (September 1, 1989). Includes a sidebar on the history of the iconic Woodstock poster.

67.   Stern, Jane, and Michael Stern. "Woodstock." *Encyclopedia of Pop Culture: An A to Z Guide of Who's Who and What's What, from Aerobics And Bubble Gum to Valley of the Dolls and Moon Unit Zappa.* New York: Harper Perennial, 1992. 567–569.

> Asserts the Woodstock Music and Art Fair represented attitudes and beliefs that still have "towering resonance." Notes the festival is still

used to benchmark the baby boomer generation's successes and failures. Recounts the difficulties in securing a location for the festival. Observes while the concert was a celebration of peace and love, many of the attendees made the journey to Bethel, New York, as a political statement. Comments the site resembled a battlefield with tents and makeshift medical accommodations.

68. Street, John. "'Invisible Republics': Making Music, Making History." *Music and Politics.* Cambridge, U.K.: Polity Press, 2012. 98–117.

Investigates the way in which music provides a perspective on history and the associate invested political meanings. Highlights two examples, the box set of recordings known as *Anthology of American Folk Music* and the Woodstock Music and Art Fair. Notes Woodstock is a prominent marker in "the mythology of music" and the festival both writes history and creates politics (i.e., politics being encoded in cultural contexts). Comments on the "notoriously fuzzy" history of Woodstock, citing conflicting data and perspectives. Observes the Woodstock festival exists today as remembered through a "multiplicity of incarnations." Surveys the life of the event on the worldwide web, mostly as utopian idealism and focused on its socio-political significance. Contrasts with the meaning ascribed by mass media, which is a shorthand for mass gatherings and/or life-changing culture happenings, a historical marker, and an aesthetic. Contrast further with the festival's debated significance in the history of rock music. Offers four narratives on the "politics of representing Woodstock" (regulatory enlightenment, radical engagement, cynical commercial exploitation, and the melding of politics and music).

69. Street, John. "This is Your Woodstock: Popular Memories and Political Myths." *Remembering Woodstock.* Ed. Andy Bennett. Aldershot, U.K.: Ashgate, 2004. 29–42.

Compares the 1969 Woodstock Music and Art Fair to the 1985 Live Aid concert in terms of political change and legacy. Begins by looking at the ways in which Woodstock continues to live "not as a historical entity, but as a multiplicity of symbols and signs." Notes the often made references to Woodstock when describing other things (e.g., Woodstock-like) in order to convey sometimes conflicting ideals. Reports on a study conducted by the author in 1999 in which college students were asked what the word "Woodstock" signaled to them. Notes responses indicated the music "seemed relatively insignificant" compared to images of the counterculture. Comments on how historical texts place varying emphasis on the Woodstock festival, if any at all. Argues Live Aid had a more significant and lasting impact on the collective political conscious. Points toward many socio-political similarities between the two concerts, but notes their legacies are quite different. Concludes the lasting mythology of Woodstock may contribute to "the history and character of popular music," but perhaps not as much to the connection between music and politics.

70. Waksman, Steve. "Popular Culture in the Public Arena." *Encyclopedia of American Cultural and Intellectual History.* v. 2. Eds. Mary Kupiec Cayton and Peter W. Williams. New York: Charle's Scribner's Sons, 2001. 143–150.

Touches quickly on Jimi Hendrix's performance of *The Star Spangled Banner* at the Woodstock Music and Art Fair. Proclaims Hendrix's rendition was "at once a supreme act of defamiliarization and a stunning political critique."

71. Weinstein, Deena. "Youth." *Key Terms in Popular Music and Culture.* Eds. Bruce Horner and Thomas Swiss. Malden, MA: Blackwell, 1999. 101–110.

Addresses questions of how vocabulary shapes one's thinking about popular music. Mentions the Woodstock Music and art Fair as having "demonstrated youth's cohesiveness as a social group defined by age" and a "myth of eternal youth." Contends the festival was as much about youth as it was rock music.

72. Whiteley, Sheila. "'1, 2, 3 what are we Fighting 4?' Music, Meaning and 'the Star Spangled Banner'." *Remembering Woodstock.* Ed. Andy Bennett. Aldershot, U.K.: Ashgate, 2004. 18–28.

Analyses Jimi Hendrix's performance of *The Star Spangled Banner* at the Woodstock Music and Art Fair from a historical perspective in order to comment on the use of music in political protest, social criticism, and especially in opposition to the Vietnam War. Introduces the Civil Rights Movement in order to contextualize the state of the urban African American experience during the 1960s. Claims the reactions to Hendrix's rendering of the national anthem and how it has come to be "considered by so many to be the most complex and powerful work of American art to deal with the Vietnam War and its effects on successive generations of the American psyche." Contends Hendrix's performance was an intentional personal statement about the turbulence of the times.

73. Wiener, Jon. "Woodstock Revisited." *The Age of Rock 2: Sights and Sounds of the American Cultural Revolution.* Ed. Jonathan Eisen. New York: Vintage Books, 1970. 170–172.

> Scrutinizes the claimed profits, or lack thereof, from the Woodstock Music and Art Fair against the actual expenses. Reports the amounts some of the musical acts were paid. Concludes the festival was not a revolutionary victory over capitalism, but instead was a success for those seeking to profit through exploitation of the counterculture. Calls for a ban on multi-day rock festivals and demands "free music in the parks every week."

74. Willis, Ellen. "Cultural Revolution Saved from Drowning." *Beginning to See the Light: Sex, Hope, and Rock-and-Roll.* Minneapolis. MN: University of Minnesota Press, 2012. 45–50. https://doi.org/10.5749/minnesota/9780816680788.001.0001

> Reprints *New Yorker* article (September 6, 1969) written by music critic, Ellen Willis, shortly after the Woodstock Music and Art Fair. Applauds the festival promoters for creating the illusion of the concert hardships as being "a capricious natural disaster rather than a product of human incompetence" resulting from their "sheer hubris." Calls for Woodstock Ventures to make its financial books public. States that the success of Woodstock was due mainly to the fact that the massive amounts of attendees were determined to enjoy themselves regardless of the conditions. Claims the rebelliousness of rock music does not automatically translate into a single unifying political agenda and "there can't be a revolutionary culture until there is a revolution." Concludes by noting rock music is "bourgeois at its core," being mass-produced and technology dependent, thus controlled by power and money.

75. Willis, Ellen. "Million Man Mirage." *The Essential Ellen Willis.* Ed. Nona Willis Aronowitz. Minneapolis, MN: University of Minnesota Press, 2014. 339–342. https://doi.org/10.5749/minnesota/9780816681204.003.0037

> Comments on how the news media's coverage of the Million Man March in 1995 reminded the author of the Woodstock Music and Art Fair. Observes during the Woodstock festival, news media ignored the "incompetence and dangerous irresponsibility of its promoters" and other significant negative social issues surrounding the event and, instead, focused on the more positive "spectacular exercise of collective will to live out a utopian moment." Acknowledges to have done the

opposite would have meant the news media missed the major story of
the event. Suggests utopian moments without a particular social vision
or goals can lead to unpredictable consequences, not all favorable.
Original published in the *Village Voice* (November 1995).

76. "Woodstock." *International Encyclopedia of the Social Sciences.* Ed.
William A. Darity. 2nd ed. v. 9. Detroit, MI: Macmillan Reference USA,
2008. 120–121.

Asserts the Woodstock Music and Art Fair is the "quintessential
symbol" of the 1960s counterculture. Provides some background on
the festival. Claims "intellectuals, the press, popular entertainment,
and the advertising industry have made Woodstock into the symbol of
the cultural and political ideals of the late 1960s." Argues the ethos of
the festival continues, citing the bands such as the Grateful Dead and
Phish who have large followings of fans evoking counterculture values
and lifestyles. Offers the annual Bonnaroo music festival as the closest
contemporary event with similarities to 1969's Woodstock festival.

77. "The Woodstock Generation and Rock Music are Dangerous to
American Culture." *Perspectives on Modern World History: Woodstock.* Ed.
Louise I. Gerdes. Detroit, MI: Greenhaven Press, 2012. 79–85.

Reprints *Wall Street Journal* article from August 28, 1969. Warns of a dire
future if hippies were to eventually take positions of power and influence.
Suggests this would be a regression that "will be at best a culturally
poorer America and maybe a politically degenerated America." Points
to the counterculture lifestyle as anarchic and thus counterproductive,
even harmful. Concludes by stating "opting for physical, intellectual and
cultural squalor seems an odd way to advance civilization." Includes a
sidebar on hippie fashion.

78.   Young, J. R. "Review of Various Artists, Woodstock." *The Pop, Rock,
and Soul Reader: Histories and Debates.* New York: Oxford University
Press, 2005. 225–227.

Attempts to "explore the interconnection between popular music,
musical techniques, current events, and social identity." Reprints
of a record "review" of the album *Woodstock: Music from the Original
Soundtrack and More.* Originally appeared in *Rolling Stone* magazine (July
9, 1970). Serves more as a commentary on the more delusional elements
of the 1960s counterculture.

Articles

79. Bernstein, Abraham. "Cultural Clash, Crash, and Cash." *English Journal* 60.6 (1971): 773–777. https://doi.org/10.2307/812992

Discourses on the concept of "clash" and its use in democracies and in the classroom. Claims democracies employ deeply held adversarial stances and contention "dressed up, perfumed, decorated, and policed into decency." Points to the Woodstock Music and Art Fair as an example of "a quarter-million sheep gathered into one place at one time, who didn't know they were being sheared, while praise and poetry arose from the young and even from the presumed enemies of the young." Describes members of the 1960s counterculture as chumps because they were merely a "means of profit, and not much more, to promoters of Woodstock and the publishers of Jerry Rubin and Abbey Hoffman."

80. Bissell, Roger E. "Will the Real Apollo Please Stand Up? Rand, Nietzsche, and the Reason-Emotion Dichotomy." *Journal of Ayn Rand Studies* 10.2 (2009): 343–369.

Evokes Ayn Rand's treatises on emulation and David Keirsey's theory of personality in order to explore the true nature of the Greek god Apollo. Notes these and other individuals think "they understand something essential about Apollo's nature and character, either in terms of philosophical aspects of his personality, his behavioral traits, or his social persona." Discusses, in particular, Rand's essay on the Woodstock Music and Art Fair participants being irrational when contrasted with the rationality of the Apollo moon mission. Concludes Apollo is "the god of extraverted intuition" because he explores the world, making connections between nature and humans "and exercising creative invention, whether artistic or theoretical."

81. Browne, Robert M. "Response to Edward P. J. Corbett, 'the Rhetoric of the Open Hand and the Rhetoric of the Closed Fist'." *College Composition and Communication* 21.2 (1970): 187–190 https://doi.org/10.2307/356560

Responds to a previous article published in this publication by questioning "how relevant is the traditional framework of rhetoric to the new forms of persuasion and action." Confesses to being "disturbed by the fact that one of the older rhetoric's chief functions has been an essentially conservative one: to keep the political system going." Points to the Woodstock Music and Art Fair, as well as the 1969 Moratorium

March on Washington, as demonstrating "new cultural styles and new politics" which utilize rhetorical strategies affirming identity. Claims rhetoric which assists in the building of a community "may well exploit means that are non-verbal, fragmentary, interlocutory, and alienating." Concludes by noting this newer style of rhetoric is a better reflection of the social unrests in the late 1960s and early 1970s.

82. Carlevale, John. "Dionysus Now: Dionysian Myth-History in the Sixties." *Arion* 13.2 (2005): 77–116.

Examines extensively the frequent use of "Dionysus and the Dionysian" as metaphor in the 1960s. Refers to Ayn Rand's commentary on the Woodstock Music and Art Fair in which she illustrates a crisis of values. Criticizes Rand's rhetoric and contents Rand's "narrative proposes yet another mythologization of the moment: Dionysus, god of unreason, has come and taken over the mind of the intellectual elite." Observes "Dionysus has a way of making the latest thing seem like the most ancient truth, of making what we have never seen seem like something we have always known or should have known."

83. Clecak, Peter. "The Revolution Delayed: The Political and Cultural Revolutionaries in America." *Massachusetts Review* 12.3 (1971): 590–619.

Discourses on the political revolutionaries of the 1960s counterculture, claiming "the new radicals possessed no clear program, no viable organization, not even a formidable constituency." Adds "they were innocent of the disastrous potentialities of moral vision insufficiently tempered by political realism." Focuses on Abbie Hoffman's attempt to articulate a "Woodstock nation." States that Hoffman saw the Woodstock Music and Art Fair as a model and "the birth of a nation." Faults Hoffman for relying on his own fashioned social myth based on the Woodstock festival phenomenon and having "no need for elaborate theory, no need for social vision, and no need for a politics of transition." Refers to Hoffman as being similar to the fictional character Holden Caufield from the novel *Catcher in the Rye*. Insists the real political revolution should not be side tracked by radicals lacking strategy.

84. Corning, Amy, and Howard Schuman. "Commemoration Matters: The Anniversaries of 9/11 and Woodstock." *Public Opinion Quarterly* 77.2 (2013): 433–454. https://doi.org/10.1093/poq/nft015

Studies the effect of commemorating the anniversaries of the Woodstock and Music and Art Fair and the terrorist attacks on September 11, 2001 on the collective memory and knowledge of each event. Examines the eighth and tenth anniversaries of 9/11 and the fortieth anniversary of the Woodstock festival. Findings suggest commemorative activities heighten the importance and knowledge of the events and breakdown along socio-economic status and ethnicity. Claims the results "offer insights into the educative and evocative roles of commemoration." Suggests commemorations that result in evoking identities may also shift collective memories.

85. "Deadline Club Protests Police use of News Photos." *The Quill* 87.6 (1999): 76.

Mentions use by New York State Police of copyrighted photographs taken during the riots that occurred at Woodstock '99. Reports objections raised by the New York City chapter of the Society of Professional Journalists.

86. Demers, Jason. "An American Excursion: Deleuze and Guattari from New York to Chicago." Theory & Event 14.1 (2011). http://dx.doi.org/10.1353/tae.2011.0007

Proposes French artist Jean-Jacques Lebel served as a connecting link between French and American political activism of the late 1960s, linking French theorists such as Gilles Deleuze and Félix Guattari to American anarchists. States Lebel attended the Woodstock Music and Art Fair with his friend Abbie Hoffman in order to liberate the festival via cutting open the fences. Offers Lebel's interpretation of liberation was necessary because capitalism was "using the youth culture industry as a means to absorb the energies of young people, diverting the movement away from political engagement." Reports Lebel realized that, more importantly, behind the capitalist were politicians wanting to dominate and control the social structure.

87. "A Discussion: 'The New Puritanism' Reconsidered." *Salmagundi* 106/107 (1995): 194–256.

Transcribes, in edited format, a discussion devoted to the Spring 1994 special issue of this journal on "The New Puritanism." Reports on one of the speakers, Jean Elshtain, being reminded of a scene from the motion picture *Woodstock* in which a male attendee, with a female companion beside him, says he looks forward to having sex at the festival with many women. Observes "then you see the young woman's face fall, as though a cloud crossed it." States "this kind of distance between the sexes is something that needs to be addressed."

88. Dreyfus, Hubert L. "Comments on Jonathan Lear's 'Radical Hope' (Harvard: 2006)." *Philosophical Studies* 144 (2009): 63–70. https://doi.org/10.1007/s11098-009-9367-9   http://escholarship.org/uc/item/60p3b5jx#page-8

> Critiques a work on the effects and responses to cultural devastation. Invokes the writings of Martin Heidegger regarding culturally marginal practices. Offers the Woodstock Music and Fair as being representative of a new cultural sensibility that "almost coalesced into a cultural paradigm" where traditionally accepted norms were temporarily marginalized to make room for more "pagan practices." Claims that if more people had recognized the hint of this as a potential cultural shift, then "a new understanding of being might have been focused and stabilized."

89. "Epidemiology of Substance Abuse at the 1994 Woodstock Music Festival." *Journal of Toxicology: Clinical Toxicology* 33.5 (1995): 503.

> Prints an abstract of a study conducted by the New York Poison Control Center intended to understand the nature and prevalence of illegal drug abuse at mass gatherings. Uses on-site interview methodology. Reports on the demographics of drug use at Woodstock '94. Concludes there was common use of multiple drugs, with marijuana being the most widespread.

90. Espen, Hal. "The Woodstock Wars." *New Yorker* August 15 (1994): 70–74.

> Writes on the eve of Woodstock '94 about its commercial nature in relation to the original Woodstock Music and Art Fair. Comments on the original festival and notes "the actuality of the ecstatic, miserable, mud-soaked, beatific chaos of Woodstock was instantly turned into a consumable media image." Offers the motion picture *Woodstock* and the triple-record album *Woodstock: Music from the Original Soundtrack and More* as examples. Observes Woodstock Ventures, this time around, planned for a tightly managed Woodstock '94 and engaged in "aggressive marketing and merchandising." Discusses how the 1969 festival was more unsuccessful commercialism rather than anti-commercialism. States an efficiently produced Woodstock '94 will not be able to capture the spirit of the original event because the hardships of the 1969 concert created sense of solidarity for the sake of survival. Concludes by noting an ongoing struggle to separate image (provided by mass media) from reality (provided by experience).

91. Ethen, Michael. "The Festival is Dead, Long Live the 'Festival'." *Journal of Popular Music Studies* 26.2–3 (2014): 251–267. https://doi.org/10.1111/jpms.12076

Points to the security issues associated with the Monterey International Pop Festival, the Woodstock Music and Art Fair, and the Altamont Speedway concert as an introduction to discussing "Woodstock Laws." Highlights the Woodstock festival's security strategies, such as self-policing, which resulted in a "calmer sense of conspiracy." Notes in the early 1970s state and local governments enacted legislation (i.e., Woodstock Laws) to ensure greater security measures for both music festival attendees and the surrounding communities. States new laws were often punitive and too severe to be honored. Details several ways in which the laws were enacted and enforced, citing specific rock music festivals. Concludes "Woodstock Laws" resulted in a movement towards crowd containment and size control, and reducing the number of days over which the festivals would occur. Asserts the most significant impact was the eventual movement of the events into sports stadiums thus generating revenue for municipalities.

92. Fiori, Umberto. "Rock Music and Politics in Italy." *Popular Music* 4 (1984): 261–277. https://doi.org/10.1017/s0261143000006255

Delves into the history of politics surrounding public performances of rock music in Italy. Observes concerns about rock music emphasizing inter-generational conflict and would "conceal and act as a substitute for the class battle." Notes when large-scale rock concerts were being increasingly organized and becoming politically aligned, the 1969 Woodstock Music and Art Fair served as the model. Claims the tribal and universality mythology of the Woodstock festival served the desired imagery that could be modeled for Italian political agendas. Explains how Italian rock festivals differed from other large European concerts by including organized activities to facilitate political debate.

93. Glass, Phyllis. "State 'Copyright' Protection for Performers: The First Amendment Question." *Duke Law Journal* 5 (1978): 1198–1232. https://doi.org/10.2307/1372113   http://scholarship.law.duke.edu/dlj/vol27/iss5/3/

Examines conflict between the media's ability to report newsworthy public performance events and an entertainer's right to protect the performance from unauthorized media distribution. Footnotes a court case in which the musician who performed *Mess Call* on his flugelhorn at the Woodstock Music and Art Fair attempted unsuccessfully to prevent the film footage from being used in a documentary. The musician sued under the New York privacy statute, but the court held "the statute was not intended to provide a cause of action for the appropriation of a professional entertainer's public performances." The court also held the documentary was a "privileged account of a newsworthy event; and that, in any case, an appropriation of a 45-second performance must be considered *de minimus* or insignificant." Concludes courts need to define newsworthiness "in a normative rather than a descriptive sense."

94.   Gutmann, David. "The Premature Gerontocracy: Themes of Aging and Death in the Youth Culture." *Social Research* 39.3 (1972): 416–448.

Expounds on the counterculture's preoccupation with death, based on the psychological resemblances between very old members of the population and members of the counterculture youth. Claims youthful ego can be only overcome by revolutionary violence of illicit drugs because they bring on an "unboundaried state which is achieved naturally in later life." Illustrates by claiming the Woodstock Music and Art Fair was a peaceful event because of marijuana and not due to the magic of love. Concludes in highly technological, secular societies youth become removed from meaningful labor by mass production and the lack of symbolic incentives to sacrifice, resulting is a spiraling towards gerontocracy.

95.   Hansen, Gary N. "Transportation Planning for a Large Special Event: The Woodstock '94 Experience." *ITE Journal* 66.4 (1996): 34–36, 38–39.

Describes in detail the transportation logistical planning used to manage traffic during Woodstock '94. Notes fifteen state and local agencies were involved in the efforts. Relates the early establishment of the goal of having no private vehicles travel to the site. Discusses all of the plan's components: parking lot operations, shuttle and charter buses, traffic volume projections, capacity analysis, policy development, signage, and towing. Reports what actually happened during the festival, such as having 100,000 more attendees than planned. Concludes the transportation planning was a success, despite minor unanticipated behaviors by the attendees.

96.   Helfrich, Ronald. "'What can a Hippie Contribute to our Community?' Culture Wars, Moral Panics, and the Woodstock Festival." *New York History* 91.3 (2010): 221–243.

Delves into the political and cultural contexts surrounding the Woodstock Music and Art Fair. Chronicles the difficulties the festival promoters had in securing a site for the event and their attempts at fostering positive community relations to that end. Describes the local political maneuvering used in attempts to stop the concert. Covers the local and state impact of the festival on elections, the legal system, and on legislation designed to prevent future large-scale events unless all issues of health, food, sanitation, crowd control, and safety are first addressed. Observes and articulates how the festival was viewed in moral terms, by both proponents and opponents. Notes "all sides in this ideological war used the same terms but gave them very different meanings." Claims the debate paralleled the larger American cultural wars of the 1960s.

97. Hill, Alfred. "Defamation and Privacy Under the First Amendment." *Columbia Law Review* 76.8 (1976): 1205–1313. https://doi.org/10.2307/1121666

Studies in-depth the areas of common law defamation regarding court decision implications. Illustrates the idea of commercial appropriation not needing to involve advertising by noting concisely a suit brought by a latrine worker at the Woodstock Music and Art Fair who was featured conspicuously in the commercial documentary motion picture *Woodstock*. Highlights the court decision that merely being filmed "performing his duties at a public event, which the festival clearly was, he would have no claim for invasion of privacy; but he would have such a claim if he was deliberately drawn out by the film makers" thus making him a performer in the film.

98. Holbrook, Emily. "Behind the Music: How Music Festival Organizers Manage the Risks of Burning Man, Lollapalooza, Coachella and More." *Risk Management* June (2011): 18+. http://www.rmmagazine.com/2011/06/01/behind-the-music/

Poses the worst example of failed music festival risk management was Woodstock '99. Observes the same conditions that affected originally the 1969 Woodstock Music and Art Fair resulted in a much different outcome in 1999. States with "oppressive heat, exorbitant food and water prices, lack of security and an insufficient number of facilities, the crowd of 200,000 turned to riot mode." Reports property damage approached $1 million and there were fights and rapes. Offers recommendations on risk management for multi-day festivals.

99. Howard, John A. "Troubled America." *Vital Speeches of the Day* 62.11 (1996): 340–343.

Prints the text of a speech by the author given to the Wisconsin Forum in Milwaukee (January 23, 1996). Calls for new political leaders who will steer the Unites States away from being a society of rights and entitlement toward "resurrecting those virtuous norms of Christendom." Claims the Woodstock Music and Art Fair was an insurrection against morality and decency. Asserts law enforcement's failure to contain illegal drug use at the festival meant the drug culture was then forever uncontrollable. Declares the concert was the "seedbed for the gangs of lawless youth that have turned cities into battlegrounds."

100. Howard, Thomas. "Moral Order and the Humanities." *Journal of General Education* 32.2 (1980): 135–148.

Considers the problem of making the humanities relevant to real world experiences, especially during periods of time in which the social order may be at risk. Theorizes "there is a fixed moral order, that tradition, convention, and law are the guardians and not the enemies of freedom, that no society can hold itself together without transcendent moral sanctions." Offers as one example the Woodstock Music and Art Fair. Reports mass media portrayed the participants as "untainted as they are with the original sin that has made capitalists and militarists and establishmentarians out of their fathers." Speculates if the festival had continued indefinitely, a social order similar to contemporary society would have established itself with capitalistic mechanisms, policing rules, and corrupt citizens.

101. Kiester, Edwin, Jr. "Woodstock and Beyond—Why?" *Today's Health* July 1970 (1970): 20–25, 59–61.

Begins with a discussion on the mythology of the Woodstock Music and Art Fair and the increase in the number of outdoor rock music festivals. Notes the real purpose of these gatherings is not for the music, which just becomes background, but to "validate, reinforce, and illuminate the culture." Compares these events to professional conferences where like-minded people gather. States the breakdown of adequate public health planning for Woodstock resulted in the creation of a New York state law governing large gatherings. Discusses the medical care provided at the festival. Suggests one reason Woodstock and other music festivals have been relatively peaceful is because law enforcement tends to be lenient regarding causal drug use, indecent exposure, etc. Offers these events tend to become nations unto themselves for the duration. Concludes these types of gatherings have a needed social role in contemporary society.

102. Kimball, Roger. "Charles Reich and America's Cultural Revolution." *New Criterion* 13 September (1994): 12+. http://www.newcriterion.com/articles.cfm/Charles-Reich---America-s-cultural-revolution-4992

Marvels at the "ridiculousness" of Woodstock '94 which was "a commemoration of the counter-culture that boasted cash machines, promotional tie-ins with Pepsi Cola, and a security force of twelve hundred." Notes the promoters were the same for both the original Woodstock Music and Art Fair and Woodstock '94, with the only difference being the first time around inexperience and bad planning prevented the festival from becoming an immediate commercial success. Contends a defining element of the 1969 event was "the arrogant sense of entitlement that presupposed the very affluence and bourgeois economic largess that it pretended to reject." Segues into a detailed commentary on Charles Reich's book from 1970, *The Greening of America*, describing it as a paean to the cultural revolution of the 1960s. Discusses the initial impact of, and responses to, the publication. Admits Reich's predictions came true, but offers the result was a catastrophe which still resides. Explains the reasoning through a detailed assessment of the work.

103. Kohl, Paul R. "Looking through a Glass Onion: Rock and Roll as a Modern Manifestation of Carnival." *Journal of Popular Culture* 27.1 (1993): 143–161. https://doi.org/10.1111/j.0022-3840.1993.11256343.x

Uses the medieval European carnival as characterized by Mikhail Bakhtin to frame a study of 1960s rock music. Carnival is described as the place where juxtapositions are eliminated and social-political hierarchy is removed. Claims the major consequence of carnival is a positive degradation and debasement. Argues that the Beatles contributed significantly to this realization. Focuses on the album *Sgt. Pepper's Lonely Hearts Club Band* and the dialectic response by Frank Zappa with the album *We're Only In It For The Money*. Asserts that the Monterey International Pop Festival, the Woodstock Music and Art Fair, and the Altamont Speedway concert most literally exemplify the "carnivalesque tradition."

104. Kozinets, Robert V. "Can Consumers Escape the Market? Emancipatory Illuminations from Burning Man." *Journal of Consumer Research* 29.1 (2002): 20–38. https://doi.org/10.1086/339919

Explores "the emancipatory dynamics of the Burning Man project" as an anti-marketing event. Uses both Disneyland and Woodstock '99 as counterpoints. Notes Woodstock '99 was "nonparticipative and based upon a mutually exploitative foundation." Contends the Burning

Man events are ideologically outside the marketplace and free from related exploitations. Reveals communal practices at Burning Man which distance "consumption from broader rhetorics of efficiency and rationality." Concludes escape from the market must be conceived of as "temporary and local."

105. "Laboratory Confirmation of Suspected Substance Abuse at the 1994 Woodstock Music Festival." *Journal of Toxicology: Clinical Toxicology* 33.5 (1995): 502.

Prints an abstract of a study conducted by the New York Poison Control Center intended to understand the nature of substance abuse at mass gatherings. Uses on-site urine samples of persons with altered mental status taken at Woodstock '94. Reports 52% of those tested revealed two or more substances. Concludes at mass gatherings the most critically ill individuals with altered mental status are likely suffering from polysubstance abuse.

106. Losavid, Keri. "EMS at Woodstock '99." *JEMS: A Journal of Emergency Medical Services* 24.11 (1999): 68–70. http://www.jems.com/articles/print/volume-35/issue-5/major-incidents/ems-woodstock.html

Explains the medical care provide for Woodstock '99. Notes the planning for emergency medical services (EMS) began eight months before the event with a mandated goal of "zero impact on the local EMS system." Describes the use and deployment of 1,200 volunteers, including doctors, nurses, and EMS personnel. Downplays the violence that occurred. Offers the lessons learned for future events are to have a dedicated security force for the medical team and to provide transportation between key points for all the volunteers (e.g., food tents, supply stations, medical facilities.

107. McGiverin, Bruce J. "Digital Sound Sampling, Copyright and Publicity: Protecting Against the Electronic Appropriation of Sounds." *Columbia Law Review* 87.8 (1987): 1723–1746. https://doi.org/10.2307/1122746

Explores sound sampling as a phenomenon where "perhaps for the first time a small aspect of a performance both is valuable and can, contrary to the policies underlying protection of performance value, undercut a performer's ability to earn a living." Footnotes a court case in which the musician who performed "Mess Call" on his flugelhorn at the Woodstock Music and Art Fair attempted unsuccessfully to prevent the film footage to be used in a documentary. Concludes that digital sound sampling is a threat but the current copyright law can handle extreme abuses.

108. "Memories of Woodstock." *Society* 27.1 (1989): 2.

Reports succinctly on results from a Gallop poll regarding the public's memories of who performed at the Woodstock Music and Art Fair. Notes nearly all rock music fans under 25 years of age can name Jimi Hendrix and Janis Joplin, as well as some other groups who have remained popular since the festival (e.g., Crosby, Stills, Nash & Young, Jefferson Airplane, The Who). Observes rock music fans over the age of 30 are more likely to remember the folk music acts (e.g., Joan Baez, Arlo Guthrie, Richie Havens, Country Joe McDonald).

109. Murchison, William. "The Worst Years of our Lives." *American Spectator* 42.8 (2009): 16–21. http://spectator.org/40806_worst-years-our-lives/

Argues on the fortieth anniversary of the Woodstock Music and Art Fair the damage inflicted by the Woodstock era on institutions and moral understandings was enormous and lasting. Implies a reason the festival is mythologized is because history is written by the winners (i.e., the counterculture baby boomers who came to control the mass media in the 1970s).

110. Nieburg, H. L. "Agonistics—Rituals of Conflict." *Annals of the American Academy of Political and Social Science* 391 (1970): 56–73. https://doi.org/10.1177/000271627039100106

Defines "agonistics" as "animal conflict behavior that is playful, symbolic, or ritualistic" and political. Suggests studying human agonistics is a legitimate area for theory and analysis, as evidenced by the Woodstock Music and Art Fair and other mass events of the 1960s. Asserts through agnostics, members of a social group "discover, learn, and communicate their place in an ordered set of relationships." Observes Woodstock, as a large group event, inverted "the normal sense of danger and the reflexes of self-protection, liberating people from their usual private roles." Offers the festival was the first mass ritual for many of the participants. Claims Woodstock served as a ritual of ceremony and a rite of passage. Offers the event changed attitudes and values without conflict, thus being "redressive, reconciling means of reaffirming loyalties, at times testing and changing them or offering new ones to replace the old." Concludes the counterculture needs to be assimilated to avoid violent power struggles. Notes the process has already begun with the lowering of the voting age and reforming the military draft system, among other actions of the time.

111. Nolan, Kenneth P. "Sorry." *Litigation* 36.1 (2009): 55–56, 58.

Starts with a description of the author's youthful journey to the Woodstock Music and Art Fair. Portrays the festival as a coming out party for a "generous, caring, peaceful" generation, yet at the same time as a hint of the excessive consumptions to come. Bemoans the evolution of the Woodstock generation into one equating happiness with material success. Claims baby boomers "were given a world where America was admired and loved" and turned it into one "where half the world wants to blow up the Statue of Liberty."

112. "Nostalgie De La Boue." *New Criterion* 13 September 1994 (1994): 2–3.

Reflects on Woodstock '94 as the heir to the original Woodstock Music and Art Fair. Describes as a fairy tale the common notion that in 1969 there was a "spirit of non-violence, anti-materialism, and brotherly love." Notes, rather, there were drug overdoses and mindless political slogans. Regardless, the mythological images from 1969 were invoked to sell Woodstock '94 to the public. Observes, in the end, Woodstock '94 did mirror the reality of the 1969 event with heavy rains, numerous drug overdoses, and an underlying profit motive. Concludes by invoking Karl Marx and suggesting the two events were "a farcical tragedy that came back as a black comedy."

113. O'Rourke, John J., and John J. Murphy Jr. "Woodstock '94: Fire Planning for Large Public Events." *Fire Engineering* 148.1 (1995): 74+. http://www.fireengineering.com/articles/print/volume-148/issue-1/features/woodstock-94-fire-planning-for-large-public-events.html

Describes the fire prevention planning for Woodstock '94. Addresses fire protection for helicopter landing pads and temporary medical care facilities. Covers such issues as maintaining an adequate water supply, haz-mat preparations, and fireworks. Mentions difficulties in acquiring appropriate funding for the mission. Recommends planning begins at inception and includes access roads and staging a command center far away from the main stage.

114. Panichas, George A. "The Woodstock in Ourselves." *Modern Age* 37.3 (1995): 194–199.

Editorializes Woodstock '94 as a negative representation of American culture because "we reveal ourselves through what we choose to celebrate." States Woodstock '94 personified and was emblematic of "that final phase in the modern age when romanticism slips into nihilism." Criticizes the news media, and the *New York Times* in particular, for ignoring the larger social implications of the event (a compilation of the New York Times article on the event is available at http://woodstockpreservation.org/Gallery/NYTCompilation.html). Compares the concert attendees to Hitler's Youth in terms of displaying similarly threatening attitudes. Concludes the lack of critique in the mass media means Woodstock '94 symbolizes spiritual emptiness, social disorientation, and moral obtuseness.

115. Peterson, Richard A. "The Unnatural History of Rock Festivals: An Instance of Media Facilitation." *Popular Music & Society* 2.2 (1973): 97–123. https://doi.org/10.1080/03007767308591005

Identifies relevant environmental factors for a proper understanding of the rock music festival phenomenon. Asserts "a combination of external economic, political, and social forces" affected negatively the viability of holding large-scale rock festivals, all fostered with the assistance of the news media. Claims problems associated with rock festivals are not necessarily a function of their great sizes. Offers the Monterey International Pop Festival as the turning point where the potential for commercial exploitation was demonstrated. Follows by providing the planning for the Woodstock Music and Art Fair as an example of promoters acting irresponsibly under concern for making a profit. Compares and contrast problems associated with urban versus rural festivals, including Woodstock, suggesting an inverse relationship. Delves into the ideological bias of the news media when covering rock music festivals. Explores the ways in which the legal system has been used to suppress festivals, through the courts, legislatures, and executive offices.

116. Rahman, Ahmad A. "The Million Man March: A Black Woodstock?" *The Black Scholar* 26.1 (1996): 41–44. https://doi.org/10.10 80/00064246.1996.11430771

Discusses unfavorable similarities between the Million Man March (1995) and the Woodstock Music and Art Fair (1969). Begins with the premise Woodstock has become no more that "a signpost on the way toward assimilation into white privilege and produced no lasting social or economic changes." Notes attending the Woodstock concert conveyed that one was opposed to the Vietnam War, favored the legalization of marijuana, and supported the Civil Rights Movement. Claims the Woodstock festival did not, however, develop into a permanent counterculture movement due to a lack of leaders willing to establish an ideology and transform the energy of the event into political action. Argues the Million Man March parallels Woodstock in being an apex of a national voice suggesting that if it follows the same history as Woodstock, it will "reveal the limitations of cultural nationalism as a guiding political philosophy for bringing about social change."

117. Rauchway, Eric. "Santa Only Brought Me the Blues: Family Holidays, Old and New." *Reviews in American History* 30.1 (2002): 98–105. https://doi.org/10.1353/rah.2002.0017

Utilizes Jimi Hendrix's performance of *The Star Spangled Banner* at the Woodstock Music and Art Fair as an example of a syncretic event. States Hendrix both asserted his "Americanness" and maintained his ethnicity "by reinterpreting a dominant cultural custom in his own idiom." Contrasts the 1969 festival with later incarnations (i.e., Woodstock '94, Woodstock '99) by offering that the original event was a holiday from the normal social order while the later ones were more carnivalesque.

118. Reeves, Richard. "Mike Lang (Groovy Kid from Brooklyn) Plus John Roberts (Unlimited Capital) Equals Woodstock." *New York Times Magazine* September 7 (1969): 34–35+.

Profiles John Roberts who provided the capital to fund the Woodstock Music and Art Fair. Discusses his relationship with Michael Lang and the other two creators of the company Woodstock Ventures. Includes some biographical information on Roberts. Delves into the finances behind the event. Quotes Roberts expressing hope of making up the losses on the festival through the release of the motion picture *Woodstock*. Includes a sidebar describing what it was like to be at Woodstock as a reporter.

119. Rodrick, Stephen. "Woodstock Postcard: Gone to Pot." *New Republic* 211.10 (1994): 9.

Comments on the overt commercialism observed at Woodstock '94.

120. Russo, Elena. "1966: Morning in Baltimore." *Romantic Review* 101.1/2 (2010): 167–189.

Draws a parallel between the Woodstock Music and Art Fair in 1969 and a symposium on "the languages of criticism and the sciences of man" held at Johns Hopkins University in 1966. The symposium included invited French nihilists. States both events were portrayed as barbarian invasions and both events continue to be discussed forty years later.

121. Salgado, Richard P. "Regulating a Video Revolution." *Yale Law & Policy Review* 7.2 (1989): 516–537. http://digitalcommons.law.yale.edu/cgi/viewcontent.cgi?article=1170&context=ylpr

> Examines retail videotape rentals of motion pictures, a relatively new phenomenon in 1989. Observes how children may now have access to movies intended for adults, thus creating pressure for legislatures "to regulate which videotapes may be distributed and to whom." Refers to a court case surrounding a statute restricting access for anyone under the age of eighteen to the motion picture *Woodstock*. Notes the "court struck down the statute on first amendment grounds as a prior restraint" because judicial supervision is "essential to the determination of whether particular speech is unprotected for the purpose of issuing a prior restraint." Reports the court found fault with the judgment made by the Motion Picture Association of America (MPAA) using unknown standards and procedures. Concludes that while legislatures may draft statutes classifying some videos inappropriate for minors, they cannot abdicate the responsibility to "private organizations which are virtually immune from judicial scrutiny," such as MPAA.

122. Samuels, David. "Rock is Dead: Sex, Drugs, and Raw Sewage at Woodstock '99." *Harper's Magazine* November (1999): 69–82.

> Attempts to make sense, in some detail, of the conditions and attitudes that led to the riots at Woodstock '99. Follows Michael Lang during the lead up to and through the event. Shows the festival unfolding through the perspective of one of the organizers, John Scher. Describes the concert as a "prepackaged Information-Age happening." Concludes the riots were the result of something greater than the sum of the parts (e.g., poor planning, greed, personal irresponsibility). Offers America has yet to recover from the breakdown in society which occurred three decades early and was symbolized by the original Woodstock Music and Art Fair.

123. Sisk, John P. "The Young and the Irreverent." *Georgia Review* 43.3 (1989): 447–457.

> Invokes the Woodstock Music and Art Fair as an example of a puerilist society in which childish behavior is observed in adults. States society corrupted by puerilism exhibits elders who "are inclined to take without question the expressed or implied social criticism of the young." Suggests Woodstock participants expressed ideas about "sex, social and political arrangements, education, interpersonal relations, and war." States the crowd at Woodstock was, in actuality, possessed by these ideas rather

than having ownership over them. Suggests Woodstock represented nothing more than a temporary irreverence, an example of secular society worshiping youth.

124. Smedinghoff, Gerry. "Deconstructing the Conservative Mind." *Vital Speeches of the Day* 71.8 (2005): 234–242. http://www.gerrysmedinghoff. com/articles/DeconstructingTheConservativeMind.pdf

> Prints a speech by the author given to the Economic Supper Club of Phoenix, Arizona (January 19, 2005). Declares time has proven the premise of the book *The Conservative Mind* by Russell Kirk to be "a self-delusional lie." Offers the German youth of the 1930s and the American counterculture youth of the 1960s as the "best example of Karl Marx's dictum that history repeats itself: first as a tragedy, then as a farce." Represents these two generations via the motion pictures *Triumph of Will* and *Woodstock* in which documented are mirror cohorts of youth expressing immature emotions and "shouting the same mindless slogans."

125. Sobieraj, Sarah, and Heather Laube. "Confronting the Social Context of the Classroom: Media Events, Shared Cultural Experience, and Student Response." *Teaching Sociology* 29.4 (2001): 463–470. https:// doi.org/10.2307/1318947   http://as.tufts.edu/sociology/sites/all/themes/ asbase/assets/documents/sobierajSocialcontext.pdf

> Asserts "student response to course content is contingent upon many factors, including the social context in which they interact with class materials." Conveys a personal example of teaching on the topic of pornography and the use of a *Time* magazine article reporting on rape at Woodstock '99. Relates students were focused more on the concept of blame being placed on the music group Korn, specifically mentioned in the article, than on the cause of the public rapes. Explores explanations for this reaction. Suggests reasons in light of recent debates on violence in media. Concludes teachers of sociology need to be mindful of the social context within the classroom in order to take advantage of important teaching moments.

126. Stahl, Gerry. "Attuned to being: Heideggerian Music in Technological Society." *Boundary 2* 4.2 (1976): 635–664. https://doi. org/10.2307/302157   http://gerrystahl.net/publications/interpretations/ attuned.pdf

> Posits contemporary art must embody a state of technology "in order to criticize its contemporary social form." Asserts it is necessary to merge Martin Heidegger's views on art with Karl Marx's critical theory on

capitalism. Applies Heidegger to a conceptualization of electronic music. Insists "art must relate to the historical context of its desired audience and appropriately interpret the truth of its own medium." Offers as a prime example Jimi Hendrix's rendering of *The Star Spangled Banner* at the Woodstock Music and Art Fair. Suggests the performance serves to comment, without words, on the United States involvement in the Vietnam War and Hendrix is "interpreting an historical text in a manner suited to a contemporary audience."

127. Torn, Jon Leon. "Taking Public Address Seriously: A Graduate Student's Response." *Rhetoric & Public Affairs* 4.3 (2001): 515–524. https://doi.org/10.1353/rap.2001.0055

Conceptualizes rock music as a combination of "the transcendence over human suffering that exemplified the blues, the truth-telling emotional power of black gospel, and the 'authentic' social critique of folk music." Notes the 1960s saw the rise of the musician as politician. Calls for more public discourse on the politics of rock music culture given the continuing "gender and racial politics of male sexual license and cultural appropriation" still in evidence. Cites the rioting and rapes at Woodstock '99 as making evident a lack of sustained progress in this area.

128. Vider, Stephen. "Rethinking Crowd Violence: Self-Categorization Theory and the Woodstock 1999 Riot." *Journal for the Theory of Social Behaviour* 34.2 (2004): 141–166. https://doi.org/10.1111/j.0021-8308.2004.00240.x

Evaluates a cognitive model of collective behavior known as Self-Categorization Theory (SCT) in order to understand crowd violence, using the riots at Woodstock '99 because they have been described as both "social protest" and "irrational delinquency." Specifically, examines "whether social identity was a significant factor in the emergence and spread of violence." Describes the physical environment and conditions at Woodstock '99. Explores motivations behind the rioting, including the use of illegal drugs. Offers there was a social purpose to the violence and some claimed the rioting was a "response to inflated prices, inadequate sanitation, and otherwise poor conditions." Notes much of the action was aimed towards property representative of the promoters and other commercial entities as opposed to other individual concert attendees. Questions whether rioting was caused by a sense of economic injustice or was extreme commercialism simply used as a justification. Suggests the reality was a "behavioral unity with cognitive diversity." Invokes Freud to describe the crowd's psychological response to violent messages emanating from the stage. Claims SCT fails to account for the "attraction and excitement" of joining a violent crowd. Compares and contrasts the

Woodstock '99 events to a riot at Ohio State University in November 2002 following a football game, suggesting tradition as a source of behavioral norms, including crowd violence. Claims the news media helps to establish ritualized memory, as in the mythology of rebellion created from the original Woodstock Music and Art Fair held in 1969.

129. Zito, Jack S. "Music Medicine." *MLO: Medical Laboratory Observer* 32.2 (2000): 40–44. https://www.thefreelibrary.com/Music+ medicine.-a060014062

Describes from a first-person perspective the management of medical services provided by Centrex Clinical Laboratories at Woodstock '99. Discusses staff coverage, drug-screening arrangements, and supplies. Notes majority of patients were treated for dehydration, drug overdoses, and mosh pit injuries.

Proceedings

130. Cunha, Victoria. "The Medium is the (Rock) Message: A Mythic Comparison of Woodstock and Live Aid." *Annual Meeting of the Speech Communication Association.* November 3–6, 1988, New Orleans, LA.

Seeks to discover a relationship between promotional media used for significant events and the nature of the post-event mythology. Compares the 1969 Woodstock Music and Art Fair with the 1985 Live Aid concert by examining the ways in which the events were organized, promoted, and executed. Although Live Aid attempted to capitalized on the Woodstock mythology, it ultimately failed due to generational and philosophical differences.

Websites

131. Mathewes-Green, Frederica. "Woodstock II: Regeneration Gap." 1994. http://frederica.com/writings/woodstock-ii-regeneration-gap.html

Uses the original Woodstock Music and Art Fair and the subsequent Woodstock '94 to comment on the differing values of the two generations (baby boomers vs. Generation X) served by the events. Notes the flaws associated with both generations and observes Generation X has "no defining passion, no idealism, no role except consumer." Explores the current fascination with Charles Manson, citing the appropriation of his cult-like status by Generation X musicians (Guns N' Roses, Evan Dando, and Trent Reznor). Describes Joe Cocker's performances at Woodstock '94. Comments on the violent stage antics of Nine Inch Nails and Blind Melon at the same event. Concludes the original Woodstock gave society "sex, drugs and rock 'n' roll" while Woodstock '94 added "rage, contempt, and meaninglessness.

132. Sanjek, David. "Woodstock", in *Encyclopedia of American Studies*. Baltimore, MD: Johns Hopkins University Press, 2010.

Describes in a few words the Woodstock Music and Art Fair from a sociological perspective. States Woodstock was a manifestation of increasing corporate investment in the 1960s counterculture. Claims "large-scale musical gatherings such as Woodstock exist simultaneously in an industrial and an ideological dimension." Asserts, therefore, events such as Woodstock force the exploration of a generation's "aims and aspirations." Touches on the failed attempts to "recapture the transient sensibilities" of 1969's Woodstock event through Woodstock '94 and Woodstock '99, noting popular music by then had become a consumer good as opposed to a "road to egalitarian aspirations." Questions where contemporary youth can express their idealized futures.

Videos

133. *The Sixties: The Years that Shaped a Generation.* Paramount Home Entertainment, 2005. https://www.youtube.com/watch?v=mUc2eLe-ruI

Features interviews with the notable persons from the 1960s, including: Daniel Ellsberg, Jesse Jackson, Tom Hayden, Arlo Guthrie, Henry Kissinger, Norman Mailer, Robert McNamara, Ed Messe, and Bobby Seale. Includes discussion of the Woodstock Music and Art Fair and the Altamont Speedway concert. Also covers the Vietnam War, the Civil Rights Movement, counterculture politics and associated events. Includes archival footage.

Photo by Mark Goff, image in the public domain. Wikimedia, https://commons.
wikimedia.org/wiki/File:Woodstock_August_15,_1969.jpg

History

Books

134. Alan, Carter. *Radio Free Boston: The Rise and Fall of WBCN*. Boston: Northeastern University Press, 2013.

Chronicles the history of radio station WBCN (Boston). Reveals briefly the role and activities of WBCN during Woodstock '94. States the radio station's experience at the concert played a major role in transforming WBCN from an AOR format to modern rock. Observes how Woodstock '94 served as a large test market for the demographics WBCN was attempting to target. Foreword by Steven Tyler.

135. Anson, Robert Sam. *Gone Crazy and Back Again: The Rise and Fall of the 'Rolling Stone' Generation*. New York: Doubleday, 1981.

Provides a history of *Rolling Stone* magazine and an examination of its cultural significance. Focuses on Jann Wenner who founded the publication in 1967 with $7,500 in borrowed capital. Recounts the highlights of the Woodstock Music and Art Festival, noting "the moment is beyond comprehension." Focuses on the peaceful nature of the event and the politeness extended to the local community by the attendees. Mentions Wenner was startled by the festival. Claims he did not think the event would be successful by any measurement. States many journalists covering the festival reported it as a new beginning, signaling a recognition of Wenner's assertions of rock music representing an anthem of new values.

136. Blake, Mark. *Pretend You're in a War: The Who and the Sixties*. London: Aurum Press, 2014.

Provides the most detailed account of The Who's experience at the Woodstock Music and Art Fair. Describes how the band demanded

     http://dx.doi.org/10.11647/OBP.0105.02

payment before taking the stage. Offers thoughts on the group having to perform at the festival immediately following Sly and the Family Stone's set. Recounts the incident of Abbie Hoffman attempting to take the stage during The Who's performance and Pete Townshend intervening by knocking him off the stage.

137. Blelock, Weston, and Julia Blelock, eds. *Roots of the 1969 Woodstock Festival: The Backstory to "Woodstock."* Woodstock, NY: WoodstockArts, 2009.

Explains why the Woodstock Music and Art Fair was named after the town of Woodstock, New York, even though the concert took place in Bethel, New York. Presents the transcript from a panel discussion (August 9, 2008) revealing how the concept for the festival developed from, and was shaped by, the legacy of art and music events associated with the community of Woodstock. Panelist included Michael Lang, Woodstock resident and one of the promoters of the 1969 Woodstock concert; Jean Young, co-author with Lang on the book *Woodstock Festival Remembered*; plus others knowledgeable about the local music scene in the late 1960s. Delves into the town of Woodstock's early arts and crafts tradition and its history of weekend-long musical concerts. Includes numerous photographs and maps.

138. Bordowitz, Hank. *Bad Moon Rising: The Unauthorized History of Creedence Clearwater Revival.* Chicago: Chicago Review Press, 2007.

Presents the story of the band Creedence Clearwater Revival. Describes how the band was signed early on, in April 1969, to play at the Woodstock Music and Art Fair. Suggests the group was used as leverage by the festival promoters to attract other acts. Quotes John Fogerty on his disappointment of playing the gig at 3:00 a.m. with the audience mostly asleep. Explains Creedence Clearwater Revival's absence from the motion picture *Woodstock* due to Fogerty's displeasure with their performance. Notes Fogerty also kept the film footage of the band out of the twenty-fifth anniversary director's cut of the film.

139. Brant, Marley. *Join Together: Forty Years of the Rock Music Festival.* New York: Backbeat Books, 2008.

Surveys the major rock music festivals held between 1967 and 2007. Attempts to portray the events as having made important contributions to society. Asserts the Woodstock Music and Art Festival came to "represent a massive sociological transformation and define a generation." Provides background on how Joel Rosenmann, John Roberts, Artie Kornfeld, and

Michael Lang (the four promoters of the original Woodstock festival) came to know each other and to eventually form Woodstock Ventures. Offers insight on securing a site for the event from farmer/businessman Max Yasgur. Mentions some of the fees negotiated to secure performers. Explains how the festival came together as a series of last minute activities and the consequences regarding traffic control, food, and security arrangements. Includes details on many of the on-stage and behind-the-scenes issues surrounding the performances and the impromptu scheduling of the opening act, Richie Havens. Incorporates the ways in which adverse weather affected the various acts and their sets. Covers some of the artists who did not play at Woodstock and the reasons why. Quotes the overall positive reflections on the festival by some of the performers. Delves into post-event financial issues facing the promoters and the eventual success of the motion picture *Woodstock*. Concludes with a discussion on the impact of the event on the music industry, performers, and subsequent music festivals. Includes sections devoted to Woodstock '79, Woodstock '89, Woodstock '94, and Woodstock '99.

140. Brown, Tony, ed. *Jimi Hendrix: In His Own Words*. London: Omnibus, 1994.

Collects excerpts from interviews with Jimi Hendrix. Notes Hendrix was "always very articulate and unafraid to express his views." Quotes selectively Hendrix's comments on the Woodstock Music and Art Fair. Hendrix mentions extensively the non-violence at the festival and extrapolates it to the larger counterculture; bemoans the lack of access to music festivals for inner city youth; and recommends future events should include a variety of activities to occupy the audience, suggesting there be films, dances, art, exhibits, and plays. Comments on his rendition of *The Star Spangled Banner* at the festival. Other topics include his time spent in the U.S. Army, songwriting, and politics.

141. Carson, David A. *Grit, Noise, & Revolution: The Birth of Detroit Rock 'n' Roll*. Ann Arbor, MI: University of Michigan Press, 2005. https://doi.org/10.3998/mpub.93680

Chronicles the Detroit music scene of the 1960s and 1970s. Describes the Woodstock Music and Art Fair from the perspective of the White Panthers and the "Free John Sinclair" movement. Tells the story of representatives from the White Panthers traveling to the festival and connecting with Abbie Hoffman. Sheds insight into Hoffman's ill-fated attempt to radicalize the audience from the stage. Reveals actual roadblocks were established to catch hippies with illegal drugs leaving the event.

142. Cooke, John Byrne. *On the Road with Janis Joplin*. New York: Berkley Books, 2014.

Describes the author's experience as road manager for Janis Joplin. Details difficulties of getting Joplin to the Woodstock Music and Art Fair due to the heavy traffic. Describes the helicopter ride from the Holiday Inn to the festival site. Provides insights to backstage happenings. Draws comparisons between 1967's Monterey International Pop Festival and 1969's Woodstock, both of which the author attended.

143. Curtis, Jim. *Rock Eras: Interpretations of Music and Society, 1954–1984*. Bowling Green, OH: Bowling Green State University Popular Press, 1987.

Utilizes Marshall McLuhan's work to organize the history of rock music into three eras. Subdivides each era into two parts, innovation and assimilation. Stresses the political environment in the second era, 1964–1974. Discusses the relationship forged between popular culture and high culture while exploring the late 1960s counterculture politics of music. Illustrates the redefining of what it meant to be an American by citing Jimi Hendrix's rendering of *The Star Spangled Banner* at the Woodstock Music and Art Fair. Discusses the creation and undermining of the Woodstock mythology of peacefulness and gentleness. Draws a connection among the Charles Manson murders, Woodstock, and the Altamont Speedway concert. Points to the contradictions between the counterculture ethos of "we are brothers and sisters" and everyone "do your own thing." Claims the Woodstock festival illustrates a key principle of McLuhan's, that "processes are not monolithic, and that they can reverse themselves." Delves into the religious parallels of Woodstock, noting the performance by Sly Stone was reflective of black gospel music given he invoked a call-and-response during the set. Suggests Woodstock provided a "lasting spirituality."

144. Davidson, Sara. *Loose Change: Three Women of the Sixties*. Garden City, NY: Doubleday, 1977.

Presents the stories of how three women, including the author, lived through the counterculture experience of the 1960s. Comments in a few words about the author's backstage experience at the Woodstock Music and Art Fair. Comments on the odor of 500,000 attendees ("rotting fruit, urine, sweat, incense"). Reports the author wrote an article about the event for *The Globe*.

145. DeGroot, Gerard J. *The Sixties Unplugged: A Kaleidoscopic History of a Disorderly Decade*. Cambridge, MA: Harvard University Press, 2008.

Offers a history of the 1960s from an atypical perspective suggesting the decade lacked a "coherent logic." Defies convention by examining the 1960s in a nonlinear fashion. Presents sixty-seven topics lacking a single narrative in order to demonstrate a more realistic and less romanticized portrayal of history. Describes the origins of the Woodstock Music and Art Fair as a money-making scheme. States the artists performing at the festival did so only due to offers of being well paid. Discusses the financial aspects of the event, but notes the post-festival mythology recast the concert as the "perfect ending to the Heavenly Decade," representing "the epitome of freedom." Suggests the mythology sustains itself because it symbolizes sentiment over a brief moment in time that was quickly destroyed by commercialism. Hints the following disastrous Altamont Speedway concert was doomed because "so many people thought Altamont was going to be like Woodstock, even though Woodstock was not really like Woodstock."

146. Draper, Robert. *The Rolling Stone Story*. Edinburgh, Scotland: Mainstream, 1990.

Offers a history of *Rolling Stone* magazine, with a focus on the individuals who helped craft the publication across time. Reports on the experience of three *Rolling Stone* reporters (Jan Hodenfield, Greil Marcus, Baron Wolman) attending the Woodstock Music and Art Fair. Provides a perspective on the festival from the impressions of counterculture journalists. Comments on the traffic and the weather. Offers the threesome came to the realization they were at an event that "defied historical precedent" and was "a triumph of the ordinary — a celebration of, by and for the masses." Notes Hodenfield's interpretation of Jimi Hendrix's rendering of *The Star Spangled Banner* as being a clarion call.

147. Evans, Mike, and Paul Kingsbury, eds. *Woodstock: Three Days that Rocked the World*. New York: Sterling, 2009.

Celebrates the 40th Anniversary of the 1969 Woodstock Music and Art Fair with a massive amount of photography accompanied by informative blocks of text and quotes. Starts with presenting in snippets the cultural events that allowed the Woodstock festival to be born (e.g., Civil Rights Movement, Vietnam War, Democratic Convention in Chicago

1968, hippies, Newport Jazz Festival, Newport Folk Festival, Monterey International Pop Festival). Continues with the events surrounding the conceptualization and realization of Woodstock. Devotes the majority of the work to the unfolding of the three days in August 1969, with a presentation of each performer's set in the same order of appearance as at the event. Mentions the reasons some of the artists who were expected to play at Woodstock did not make it. Includes a section on the aftermath (the media, the film, the money trail, and some subsequent music festivals). Ends with a "where are they now" piece and a discography. Contains annotated timelines (pre-Woodstock, from 1954 to 1969; post-Woodstock, from 1969 to 1975) and a bibliography. Foreword by Martin Scorsese.

148. Evers, Alf. *The Catskills: From Wilderness to Woodstock*. Garden City, NY: Doubleday, 1972.

Details the history of New York's Catskills Mountains. Suggests some of the residents of Sullivan County, site of the Woodstock Music and Art Fair, were receptive to hosting the festival as a means of shedding its "Borscht Belt image." Provides a local perspective on the festival. Claims during Woodstock many of the residents "lived in fear, cut off from the rest of their world by a restless sea of 400,000 young people." Notes after the event, Bethel, New York, citizens had the town supervisor removed from office. Reports the town's Postmaster, Richard Joyner, lost twenty pounds during the three-day weekend. Explains how the festival came to be named after the New York town of Woodstock, relating the community's history as an artists' colony. States one result of the concert was the ability of local resorts to more easily promote the region.

149. Evers, Alf. *Woodstock: History of an American Town*. Woodstock, NY: Overlook Press, 1987.

Details the long history of Woodstock, New York, including its evolution into an artists' community. Mentions concisely how Woodstock Ventures managed a "brazen theft of the town's name" for the Woodstock Music and Art Fair. Notes many of those hoping to attend the festival ended up first arriving at this town only to be told the event was sixty miles away. Offers insight into relationships among the community, tourism, and the hippie culture of the 1960s.

150. Fornatale, Pete. *Back to the Garden: The Story of Woodstock*. New York: Touchstone, 2009.

Represents scores of first-person accounts of the Woodstock Music and Art Fair, focusing mainly on the music and musicians while placing the festival within a cultural context. Contends Woodstock redefined "the culture, the country, and the core values of an entire generation." Organizes chapters chronologically by each performance. Describes the various narratives as "blind men and women trying to describe this behemoth based on the part of the body that we touched." Invoking the Rashomon effect, contends that despite differing experiences and descriptions of the same weekend in August 1969, some of which are "wildly divergent" and "diametrically opposed," it is true "each account can still be plausible" because each person's experience is the reality of the event for them. References Joseph Campbell, asserting "Woodstock made us feel the rapture of being alive." Foreword by Country Joe McDonald.

151. Francese, Carl, and Richard S. Sorrell. *From Tupelo to Woodstock: Youth, Race, and Rock-and-Roll in America, 1954–1969*. Dubuque, Iowa: Kendall/Hunt, 1995.

Contributes little new to the subject matter, but this textbook does place the Woodstock Music and Art Fair within the context of the social history of American youth during the 1950s and 1960s. States the festival demonstrated one of the "central tenets" of the time, "civilization was evil and people (young ones, at least) would behave better in some primal state of nature." Mentions briefly as an epilogue the Woodstock '94 and Woodstock '99 concerts.

152. Friedlander, Paul. *Rock and Roll: A Social History*. Boulder, CO: Westview Press, 2006.

Chronicles the first fifty years of rock music. Mentions Woodstock '94 was intended to be a marriage and celebration of two eras, the 1960s and the 1990s, with the former representing the mythology of community while the latter represented unashamed capitalism. Describes the rock music festival environment as it existed in the 1990s (e.g., Lilith Fair). Describes the violence at Woodstock '99.

153. Gelfand, H. Michael. *Sea Change at Annapolis: The United States Naval Academy, 1949–2000*. Chapel Hill, NC: University of North Carolina Press, 2006. https://doi.org/10.5149/9780807877470_gelfand

Recounts the most recent fifty year history (1949–2000) of the United States Naval Academy at Annapolis. Explores the people and events in relation to the Naval Academy's attempt to transform itself during changing times in order to remain relevant to midshipmen. Relates pithily a report from some students who attended the Woodstock Music and Art Fair. Notes "one thing that the weekend proved was the

Midshipmen are human and can get along with civilian college students, as long as the civilians do not know they are Midshipmen." Includes a Foreword by Senator John McCain.

154. Gerdes, Louise I., ed. *Perspectives on Modern History: Woodstock.* Detroit, MI: Greenhaven Press, 2012.

Aims toward high school and college students by presenting an anthology of twenty-three edited reprints from a wide range of original sources. Organized into three sections: historical background, controversies, and personal narratives. Introduces the topic through an exploration of the significance of the event. Notes the cultural symbolism is "perplexing to many" considering the numerous conflicting stories of what happened during those three days in August 1969. Questions some of the mythology surrounding the event, pointing out "the festival was free because of exigent circumstances, not benevolence." Contends "what actually happened at Woodstock is less important that what it means." Includes a chronology of relevant Woodstock-related events from 1966 through 2009.

155. Gittell, Myron. *Woodstock '69: Three Days of Peace, Music & Medical Care.* Kiamesha Lake, NY: Load N Go Press, 2009.

Recreates, from "sketchy" documentation and the memories of others, the numerous problems faced by medical personnel at the Woodstock Music and Art Fair. Observes that more than 3,000 attendees required medical care, thus making the festival "one of the significant disaster scene in modern America." Discusses the preparations and volunteers, the role of the Hog Farm, and the use of helicopters to airlift patients from the site. Reprints numerous primary documents related to the medical conditions at the event. Includes a statement issued immediately following the event by Max Yasgur, owner of the farm where the festival was held, stating if the festival attendees "could turn such adverse conditions, filled with the possibility of disaster, riot, looting and catastrophe into three days of peace and music, then perhaps there is hope" for a brighter future. The author, now a Registered Nurse, was at the concert but only as a spectator and not as a medical professional.

156. Green, Jonathon. *All Dressed Up: The Sixties and the Counterculture.* London: Jonathan Cape, 1998.

Traces the rise and fall of the 1960s counterculture. Refers in brief to the Woodstock Music and Art Fair as a paradigm spawning the concept of a "Woodstock nation," a fantasized alternative culture based on a single "supreme counter-culture feelgood event."

157. Harris, Craig. *The Band: Pioneers of Americana Music*. Lanham, MD: Rowman & Littlefield, 2014.

Examines the influences on the music made by The Band as well as the group's impact on the popular music of their time. Looks at The Band's appearance at the Woodstock Music and Art Fair. Provides some background with quotes from Michael Lang, one of the promoters. Lang describes the difficulties in securing a site for festival. Artie Kornfeld, another promoter, gives insight into how he and Lang evolved the concept for the event. Robbie Robertson articulates why the Woodstock concert was not the best venue for highlighting The Band's style.

158. Havers, Richard, and Richard Evans. *Woodstock Chronicles*. New York: Chartwell Books, 2009.

Contains information on the performers at the Woodstock Music and Art Fair, including short biographies, brief descriptions of their Woodstock performances, and summaries of the "Woodstock effect" on their careers. Includes a brief history of music festivals leading up to Woodstock and provides a festival chronology listing the performers at each event. Itemizes the amount each Woodstock artist was paid for their appearance. Heavily illustrated with photographs of performers and artifacts, many not from the event itself. Ends with sections on the aftermath, the albums, the film, and Woodstock '94.

159. Hillstrom, Kevin, and Laurie Collier Hillstrom. *Defining Moments: Woodstock*. Detroit, MI: Omnigraphics, 2013.

Provides an extensive accounting of the Woodstock Music and Art Fair. Targets middle and high school students. Includes a narrative overview, short biographies of ten key individuals (e.g., Michael Lang, Max Yasgur), and selections from primary sources (e.g., Ayn Rand's 1969 essay "Apollo and Dionysus"), thus making this work a comprehensive launching point for anyone researching the phenomenon. Places Woodstock within the larger context of 1960s America (e.g., Civil Rights Movement, Vietnam War, rise of the counterculture) and the role of music in shaping society during that time period (e.g., Bob Dylan, The Beatles). Examines how the festival influenced an evolving popular music culture "both as a business and as an art form." Explores the "enduring symbolic significance" of Woodstock. Presents a glossary of people, places, and vocabulary. Also includes some photographs and a chronological timeline of relevant events from 1945 (the beginning of a strong economic growth in the U.S.) to 1999 (Woodstock '99). Contains the lyrics to Joni Mitchell's song *Woodstock*. "Defining Moments" is a series of books by Omnigraphics designed to highlight significant events from American history.

160. Hoskyns, Barney. *Across the Great Divide: The Band and America.* New York: Hyperion, 1993.

> Presents a history of The Band, from 1957 through 1992. Describes the group's experience at the Woodstock Music and Art Fair. Comments on the reception of their performance. Notes the band's manager, Albert Grossman, refused to allow any of his acts at the festival (i.e., The Band, Janis Joplin, and Blood, Sweat & Tears) to be included in the motion picture *Woodstock* or on the album soundtrack. Suggest the motivation was at first financial, then vindictive towards John Roberts because of his refusal to sell the film rights to Grossman. Speculates on the career trajectory of The Band had they been included in the media products. Includes a discography.

161. Hoskyns, Barney. *Beneath the Diamond Sky: Haight Ashbury 1965–1970.* New York: Simon and Schuster, 1997.

> Presents a history of San Francisco's Haight-Ashbury hippie culture of the 1960s. Contends the tenor of the Woodstock Music and Art Fair was established by the acts from San Francisco. Claims although Janis Joplin and the Grateful Dead performed poorly at the festival, sets by Sly and the Family Stone and Santana gave "acid rock the multiracial, Afro-Latin-American jolt it needed."

162. Jahn, Mike. *Rock: From Elvis Presley to the Rolling Stones.* New York: Quadrangle, 1973.

> Attempts to convey a "complete overview of the rock age." Errors on the side of including only information about artists who contributed to the ongoing development of the genre, as opposed to those who "simply made money playing it." Offers the Woodstock Music and Art Fair as the zenith of the youth culture movement of the 1960s, after which "the downhill path was swift and straight." Attributes part of the Woodstock phenomenon to the "back to nature" movement and the growth in popularity of country rock music as evidenced by Bob Dylan's *Nashville Skyline* album, as well as recordings by Joan Baez, The Byrds, and Crosby, Stills, Nash & Young. Quotes an article from *Rolling Stone* magazine declaring Woodstock had given birth to a "new nation." Mentions the audience-engaging performance by Sly and the Family Stone as a highlight of the festival in which the communal aspects of the event were most realized. Includes a selective discography of representative music.

163. Joseph, Peter. *Good Times: An Oral History of America in the Nineteen Sixties.* New York: Charterhouse, 1973.

Based on Stud Turkel's *Hard Times: An Oral History of the Great Depression,* the author "attempts to recapture the tone and the texture" of the 1960s, if not exact facts and precise recollections. Quotes Jerry Garcia's comments on the Grateful Dead's experience at the Woodstock Music and Art Fair. Notes there were too many distractions for the band to play very well (e.g., the weather, the crowds, backstage problems). Also includes comments from Zodiac (Michael Alan Carl), providing an attendee's perspective from one of Ken Kesey's Merry Pranksters.

164. Lifton, Robert Jay. *Home from the War.* New York: Simon and Schuster, 1973.

Investigates the personal impact on veterans of having been soldiers during the Vietnam War. Claims the Woodstock Music and Art Fair had "a very special meaning for young Americans who fought in Vietnam." Relates how one veteran gained insight into "ways of living" from watching performances by Joan Baez and Richie Havens in the motion picture *Woodstock,* specifically by understanding how to enable one's ability to live their convictions.

165. Makower, Joel. *Woodstock: The Oral History.* 40th anniversary ed. Albany, NY: State University of New York Press, 2009.

Details the Woodstock Music and Art Fair through scores of interviews conducted in 1988 with "producers, performers, doctors, cops, neighbors, shopkeepers, carpenters, electricians, lawyers, journalists, filmmakers, and an assemblage of just plain folks who, by design or circumstance, became part of the event." Notes a common thread in which most people interviewed seem to date their life using the festival as a major milestone. Topics range from art and politics to life and death; and from generosity and greed to enlightenment and disenchantment. Foreword by festival producers Michael Lang and Joel Rosenman. "Who's Who" section contains brief descriptions of key participants and their relevance to the concert. Includes a detailed subject index.

166. Manchester, William. *The Glory and the Dream: A Narrative History of America, 1932–1972.* Boston, MA: Little, Brown & Co., 1974.

Focuses succinctly on the relative positive outcome of the Woodstock Music and Art Fair regarding the relatively peaceful August weekend despite rain, traffic jams, poor sanitary conditions, and lack of food, water, and medical supplies. Notes the success came mainly from members of the counterculture in the form of Ken Kesey's Merry Pranksters and the Hog Farm commune providing essential services. Claims the festival was a "strong symbol of generational unity."

167. Marcus, Daniel. *Happy Days and Wonder Years: The Fifties and the Sixties in Contemporary Cultural Politics*. New Brunswick, NJ: Rutgers University Press, 2004.

> Examines nostalgia and its effect on the narrative of history. Contends popular culture images have been used to reshape memories to fit political agendas. Points to the use by news media in the 1980s of film clips from the 1969 Woodstock Music and Art Fair as clichéd symbolism to quickly characterize the 1960s. Observes the "Sixties increasingly came to be represented by some of its most extreme and dramatic moments." Notes "events like Woodstock remained as symbols of another age, a measure of the distance the nation had traveled since the 1960s." Claims the media portrayed the 1960s as a hedonism that gave birth to the societal problems of the 1980s, such as widespread illegal drug use and sexually transmitted diseases. Considers the news media in the 1980s was often critical of the 1960s, yet the accompanying images may have been communicating an idealized, communal harmony.

168. Marcus, Greil. *Woodstock*. San Francisco, CA: Straight Arrow, 1969.

> Chronicles, in detail, the Woodstock Music and Art Fair. Captures the event immediately after it happened and, thus, presents a unique perspective from that moment in time. Observes the festival "defied categories and conventional perceptions." Describes both the music and the chaotic experiences of the attendees (e.g., problems with traffic, first-aid provision, drugs, food, sanitation, and weather). Comments on many of the performances. Notes how at Woodstock "thousands were able to do things that would ordinarily be considered rebellious" but were, instead, done for pure fun. Offers numerous black and white photographs by Baron Wolman, Joseph Sia, and Mark Vargas; a cover photo by Jim Marshall; and an overall design by Robert Kingsbury.

169. McNally, Dennis. *A Long Strange Trip: The Inside History of the Grateful Dead*. New York: Broadway Books, 2002.

> Presents a detailed and extensive history of The Grateful Dead. Describes the music group's performance at the Woodstock Music and Art Fair as "one of their worst ever." Notes problems with both the stormy weather and the electrical grounding on the stage resulted in band members being shocked from the microphones. Mentions the group's members

were intimidated by the size of the event and unprepared to deliver the spectacular show required of such a large audience. Provides a brief description of how the festival came to be organized. Describes the living arrangements for the festival performers at the nearby Holiday Inn. Sheds light on the backstage interactions and behind-the-scenes dealings. States The Grateful Dead were paid $2,250 for their performance.

170. Perone, James. *Woodstock: An Encyclopedia of the Music and Art Fair.* Westport, CT: Greenwood Press, 2005.

Presents information on all three official Woodstock festivals, concentrating heavily on the 1969 event. Uses the first half of the book to publish four essays. The first chapter covers other music festivals of the late 1960s and early 1970s, including the Monterey International Pop Festival, Newport Jazz Festival, Isle of Wight, Altamont Speedway, Newport Folk Festival, Concert for Bangladesh, and even the Beatles' rooftop concert from January 1969. The second and largest chapter discusses in detail the 1969 Woodstock Music and Art Fair. Explores the organization and planning, the demographics of the audience, use of illegal drugs, and, quite substantially, the music. Explains how the event originated as a plan to raise funds in order to build a recording studio in Woodstock, New York. Describes Woodstock Ventures as "Andy Hardy meets Rube Goldberg." Presents a statistical breakdown of the attendees, such as 55% male and 95% white. Offers some thoughts on the legacy of the original Woodstock event. The next two chapters examine in similar ways Woodstock '94 and Woodstock '99 respectively. Delves into some detail regarding the violence at Woodstock '99. The remainder of the work comprises the encyclopedic section, probably the most exhaustive attempt to-date from any publisher. Entries consist mainly of individuals, but also address many other items such as "nudity," "helicopters," and "yoga exercises." Appendices include set lists and the identification of relevant recordings and films. Closes by presenting a lengthy bibliography with brief annotations, including numerous popular magazine articles covering all three Woodstock events.

171. Pollock, Bruce. *When the Music Mattered: Rock in the 1960s.* New York: Holt, Rinehart & Winston, 1983.

Offers personal stories from individuals who played some part in the evolution of rock music during the 1960s. Marty Balin of Jefferson Airplane recalls playing poker at the Holiday Inn prior to be helicoptered to the site of the Woodstock Music and Art Fair. Essra Mohawk claims she was scheduled to perform at Woodstock but was unable to take the stage for a variety of reasons. Recounts the story of how Bob Dylan was rumored to possibly appear at the festival. States Woodstock was "more discomfiting than euphoric, except in retrospect." Describes the event as the last showing of the counterculture revolution. Paints John Sebastian's role at Woodstock as being the ideal representative of the hippie movement. Notes Sebastian was not originally scheduled to perform and took the stage under the influence of drugs. Quotes Sebastian commenting on how commercialism devoured and "cannibalized a lot of things that could have happened out of Woodstock." Reports Sebastian regrets his weak performance at the festival, especially since it was filmed and recorded for posterity.

172. Reynolds, Susan, ed. *Woodstock Revisited: 50 Far Out, Groovy, Peace-Loving, Flashback-Inducing Stories from those Who were there.* Avon, MA: Adams Media, 2009.

Remembers the 1969 Woodstock Music and Art Fair from the personal perspectives of fifty participants. Provides more than descriptions of specific happenings by articulating "what was going on in the minds of those hardy souls who traveled to Woodstock, and thus what was going on in our nation." Notes these stories reflect collectively American youth culture at the time. The editor describes this anthology as "a fascinating mixture of history, humor, and passion." Each essay is brief and written in the first person. Includes contributions from Lisa Law (of the Hog Farm), who contends the people in attendance were the festival more so than was the music. Others describe, for example, the tribulations of traveling to the concert and their resourcefulness in managing the three days of the event. Includes an eclectic "Woodstock Glossary" and four pages of "Woodstock Stats" (e.g., estimated percentage of festival attendees smoking marijuana, 90; number of portable toilets, 600).

173. Robins, Wayne. *A Brief History of Rock, Off the Record.* New York: Routledge, 2008. https://doi.org/10.4324/9780203941058

Contains a typical shorthand description of the Woodstock Music and Art Fair. States the festival represented the end of an aesthetic era and resulted in the beginning of the exploitation of rock music as a commodity which affected significantly programming at radio stations. Includes an annotated discography of essential recordings.

174. Rogan, Johnny. *Crosby, Stills, Nash & Young: The Visual Documentary.* London: Omnibus Press, 1996.

Reports on the history of Crosby, Stills, Nash & Young using a date-by-date chronological approach. Includes an entry for August 18, 1969, the day they played at the Woodstock Music and Art Fair. Notes their intimidation on playing before such a large audience. States Neil Young did not join the others on stage until later in the set. Observes Young's relative detachment during the performance. Claims their success at the festival was due more to the "empathy they displayed towards the audience, articulating and reflecting its ideals in everything from dress to political pronouncements." Articulates how their name became synonymous with the event. Includes numerous photographs, an annotated discography, and a list of unreleased compositions.

175. Santelli, Robert. *Aquarius Rising: The Rock Festival Years*. New York: Delta, 1980.

Depicts the rock festival phenomenon of the late 1960s and early 1970s. Contends the festivals "symbolized the temporary triumph" of the counterculture. Cover the Woodstock music and Art Fair from the very beginning of when John Roberts and Joel Rosenman first met, when Artie Kornfeld and Michael Lang first met, and the coming together of the foursome to formulate the concept of the Woodstock festival as a business venture. Explains issues with the initial concert location of Wallkill, New York. Reviews working relationship of the promoters and Max Yasgur, describing how his property was eventually secured for the event. Details traffic problems associated with attendees getting to the site. Highlights involvement of the Hog Farm commune in helping keep the festival from becoming a disaster. Chronicles tribulations of musicians contending with poor weather and provides notes on their performances. Highlights the acts Sly and the Family Stone and The Who. Mentions the tenor of the news media coverage, issues surrounding food availability, and medical care afforded to those having bad drug-induced experiences. Provides post-event information, including comments on the success of the motion picture *Woodstock*. Contains a partial list of the fees paid to each act.

176. Sheehan, Rita J., *Bethel*. Charleston, SC: Arcadia, 2009.

Includes archival photographs of sites from around Bethel, New York, and associated with the Woodstock Music and Art Fair.

177. Spitz, Robert Stephen. *Barefoot in Babylon: The Creation of the Woodstock Music Festival, 1969*. New York: Viking Press, 1979.

Declares the Woodstock Music and Art Fair to have been an "unprecedented historical event that spanned the generation gap and prompted a culturally divided nation to reassess its inherited morality." Strives to uncover the motivating forces that created the event and the genesis of its magnetism. Attempts to substitute the now mythological visions of Woodstock with one of a vast commercial enterprise during a period of idealism. Includes a lengthy list of individuals and their associations with the festival and a detailed site map. Provides an exhaustive history of the event, starting with the formation of Woodstock Ventures, and a blow-by-blow account of the full three days of the music festival. Focuses on the idiosyncrasies and motivations of the individual players in order to highlight the "fascinating cornucopia of personality that became the very essence" of the historical event. Details the messy financial aftermath. Concludes with a where-are-they-now section.

178. Stradling, David. *Making Mountains: New York City and the Catskills.* Seattle, WA: University of Washington Press, 2007.

Explores the relation between New York City and the Catskills Mountains. Provides a succinct accounting of the Woodstock Music and Art Fair from the perspective of its invasiveness on the New York state countryside. Focuses on the traffic and parking. Quotes dairy framer Clarence Townsend complaining of the "human cesspool" made of his property. Claims the event was a success simply because it could have been much worse. Concludes discussion of the festival by lamenting "once again the city had come to the country, as it is wont to do; it had made a mess, and then gone home." Points out Woodstock was not homegrown, but rather forced upon the locality.

179. Szatmary, David P. *Rockin' in Time: A Social History of Rock-and-Roll.* Upper Saddle River, NJ: Prentice Hall, 2010.

Places the social history of rock music within a context of American culture using a textbook format. Claims the Woodstock Music and Art Fair represented a collective antiauthoritarian attitude among America's youth. Focuses on the performances by Country Joe McDonald and Jimi Hendrix in order to illustrate the political, and even militant, nature of the festival. Asserts the soon to follow Altamont Speedway concert "dashed any sense of power that Woodstock had engendered," only to be further destroyed by the May 1970 Kent State campus shootings of students by the National Guard.

180. Tamarkin, Jeff. *Got a Revolution! The Turbulent Flight of Jefferson Airplane.* New York: Atria, 2003.

Presents a history of the musical group Jefferson Airplane. Mentions briefly the band's experience of being at the Woodstock Music and Art Fair. Notes the group elected to not allow their performance to be included in the motion picture *Woodstock*.

181. Walker, Michael. *Laurel Canyon: The Inside Story of Rock-and-Roll's Legendary Neighborhood*. New York: Farber & Farber, 2006.

Relays the history of Laurel Canyon in its heyday of being a mecca for the Los Angeles music scene from 1964 to 1981. Reports Laurel Canyon was represented at the Woodstock Music and Art Fair by Crosby, Stills, Nash & Young (CSN&Y) and Canned Heat. Notes CSN&Y rehearsed for the festival at a house in the canyon rented by Stephen Stills and owned by Peter Tork of The Monkees. Mentions David Geffen getting Warner Bros. to use the CSN&Y recording of Joni Mitchell's song "Woodstock" in the closing credits of the motion picture *Woodstock*. Contrasts the positive spirit of Woodstock with the disastrous Altamont Speedway concert taking place a few months later and held to high expectations generating from the overall positive Woodstock festival. States Woodstock and Altamont were, despite the mythology, separated only by "luck and marginally better planning."

182. *Woodstock: The 35th Anniversary (1969 Special Edition Reprint)*. [s.l.]: Life, 2004.

Serves primarily as a photographic essay documenting the original Woodstock Music and Art Fair. Includes some textual content. Originally published in 1969 as a special edition of *Life* magazine.

183. *Woodstock Music & Art Fair. Three Days of Peace and Music*. Concert Hall Publications for Woodstock Ventures Inc., 1969.

Serves as the official program book for the Woodstock Music and Art Fair (August 15–17, 1969).

184. Young, Jean, and Michael Lang. *Woodstock Festival Remembered*. New York: Ballantine Books, 1979.

Remembers the Woodstock Music and Art Fair from the perspective of Michael Lang, "the man who conceived and planned it." Attempts to provide readers with a sense of the experience from Lang's perspective, starting with the initial concept through the planning and preparations to the financial aftermath and dealings with Warner Bros. over the motion picture. Notes the first three acts booked for the festival were Jefferson Airplane, Canned Heat, and Creedence Clearwater Revival for $10,000 each. Provides insights to the efforts put towards wrangling the performers and managing the personalities behind the scenes (e.g., Abbie Hoffman). Offers the event was successful because of how it unfolded beyond anyone's imagination, "it happened spontaneously, and so folks had to react to it naturally." Reflects on the culture of the times that allowed the festival to become a historic milestone. Observes how the Hog Farm commune set the peaceful and cooperative tone for the weekend. Heavily illustrated with both color and black and white photographs.

Chapters

185. Aronowitz, Alfred G. "1969: Benign Monster Devoured Music." *American Datelines: Major News Stories from Colonial Times to the Present.* Eds. Ed Cray, Jonathan Kotler, and Miles Beller. Urbana, IL: University of Illinois Press, 2003. 339–341.

> Reprints first-person account of the Woodstock Music and Art Fair by a *New York Post* correspondent. Refers to the massive crowd as a "monster," describing it as benign, magnificent, and kept alive by the magic of music. Questions from the perspective of leaving by helicopter at the end of the event whether one would remember more the monster or its footprint.

186. Bass, Amy. "Whose Broad Stripes and Bright Stars?" *Not the Triumph but the Struggle: The 1968 Olympics and the Making of the Black Athlete.* Minneapolis, MN: University of Minnesota Press, 2002. 291–348.

> Offers a history of the African-American athlete. Argues one must "consider culture as a primary vehicle for understanding national identity." Evokes both Jose Feliciano and Jimi Hendrix as performers of controversial versions of the nation anthem. Describes Hendrix's performance of *The Star Spangled Banner* at the Woodstock Music and Art Fair as a deconstruction in which he critiqued and "dismantled the central ideas and mythologies of the United States" in an attempt at redemption. Asserts Hendrix performed a celebration, elegy, and dirge in a single instance. Equates this act at Woodstock with the black power salutes by Tommie Smith and John Carlos at the 1968 Olympics, both representative of "performative nationalism." Discusses the historic need for African Americans to use alternative methods of protest.

187. Bernstein, Jacob. "The Woodstock Festival is Now More Myth than Reality." *Perspectives on Modern World History: Woodstock.* Ed. Louise I. Gerdes. Detroit, MI: Greenhaven Press, 2012. 122–128.

> Claims news media did not initially consider the 1969 Woodstock Music and Art Fair newsworthy. Reveals *New York Times* reporter Barnard Collier was at the event "on his own dime" and the Associated Press sent 19-year-old intern Lawrence Kramer to the festival as his first

photography assignment (the photographs were published in *Life* magazine). Acknowledges the press reversed quickly this attitude, but has since overcompensated with attention and enthusiasm across time thus contributing to Woodstock's mythological status. Includes a sidebar of memorable Woodstock quotes.

188. Budds, Michael J., and Marian M. Ohman. "The Woodstock Nation." *Rock Recall: Annotated Readings in American Popular Music from the Emergence of Rock and Roll to the Demise of the Woodstock Nation.* Needham Heights, MA: Ginn Press, 1993. 292–295.

Contains reprints of items written about the Woodstock Music and Art Fair: "As Reported in the Pages of a Regional Newspaper" (*Denver Post*, August 18, 1969); "As Recalled by Participant David Crosby" (*Woodstock: The Oral History*, 1989); and "The Message of History's Biggest Happening" (*Time*, August 29, 1969). All of the items attempt to derive meaning, either cultural or personal, from the event. The book, as a whole, consists of numerous reprints and annotations that provide context through a history of writings on rock music. Emphasizes first-person accounts by performers and influential persons from behind the scenes.

189. Cavett, Dick. "The Dick Cavett show Interview (September)." *Hendrix on Hendrix: Interviews and Encounters with Jimi Hendrix.* Ed. Steven Roby, 2012. 219–225.

Transcribes Jimi Hendrix's interview on *The Dick Cavett Show* (September 9, 1969). Hendrix comments on the Woodstock Music and Art Fair, his performance of *The Star Spangled Banner*, and the lack of violence at the festival. Watch the video at: http://www.historyvshollywood.com/video/jimi-hendrix-interview-dick-cavett-show/

190. Coates, Norma. "If Anything, Blame Woodstock: The Rolling Stone — Altamont, December 6, 1969." *Performance and Popular Music: History, Place and Time.* Ed. Ian Inglis. Aldershot, U.K.: Ashgate, 2006. 58–69.

Argues the underground and mainstream press created an untrue representation of the 1960s counterculture and was "willfully blind to the practical realities of rock music" culture, leading to the tragedy at the Altamont Speedway concert. Claims the immediate mythology of the Woodstock Music and Art Fair, created by the news media, made the inadequate and loose construct of the Altamont Speedway concert inevitable. Cites overall bad publicity associated with large-scale music festivals prior to the Woodstock event, making the case that Woodstock was the exception to the rule. Scrutinizes in detail how mass media essentially forced the conditions at Altamont. Focuses to a large extent on *Rolling Stone* magazine and rock critic Ralph Gleason.

191. Collier, Barnard L. "Woodstock Participants were Peaceful and Community-Minded." *Perspectives on Modern World History: Woodstock.* Ed. Louise I. Gerdes. Detroit, MI: Greenhaven Press, 2012. 86–93.

Reproduces the *New York Times* (August 17, 1969) article from which excerpts were read from the stage to the crowd at the 1969 Woodstock Music and Art Festival. Presents Woodstock in an overall favorable light. Observes that despite the poor conditions (drenching rain and shortages of food, water, and medical facilities), the participants were well behaved, even according to the police. Continues by discussing the doctors summoned from New York City, the parked automobiles blocking the highways, the piles of garbage, and the size of the police force comprised from various agencies. Notes most of the attendees could not see the performances nor hear the music very well.

192. Cooke, Alistair. "Dire Prophecies before, and High Spirits during, Woodstock." *Perspectives on Modern World History: Woodstock.* Ed. Louise I. Gerdes. Detroit, MI: Greenhaven Press, 2012. 67–71.

Pulls from the U.K. newspaper, *The Guardian* (August 18, 1969), an article from immediately following the Woodstock Music and Art Fair (available at https://www.theguardian.com/theguardian/2010/aug/19/woodstock-music-art-fair). Indicates the fears were mostly exaggerated regarding what could possibly happen with so many from the counterculture gathering in one location (i.e., "wholesale pot smoking at best, heroin at worst, an ocean of garbage, universal bad manners, an orgy of love-ins, and probably a bloody encounter with the police"). Includes a sidebar on Jimi Hendrix.

193. Cooke, Douglas. "Woodstock Music and Art Fair 1969: Three Days of Peace and Music." *Perspectives on Modern World History: Woodstock.* Ed. Louise I. Gerdes. Detroit, MI: Greenhaven Press, 2012. 15–29.

Summarizes the Woodstock Music and Art Fair, the associated controversies, and impact of the event. Food shortages, sanitation issues, and extreme weather created an initial reaction in many of viewing the festival as a disaster. Reports the event was considered to be "a monument to faulty planning, a testament to the limitations and hypocrisies of hippie idealism, a nightmare of absurdities, ironies, and incongruities." Notes later analysis of the communal spirit, generated at the event out of necessity in the face of disaster, raised the festival to its iconic stature. Touches on the tensions between the commercial motivations behind Woodstock and the lingering mythological status it holds within American culture. Observes the anniversary event, Woodstock '94, "reflected the apathy and passive consumption" associated with Generation X.

194. Cullen, Jim. "Woodstock Music Festival Marks the Climax of 1960's Youth Culture." *Great Events from History.* Ed. Robert F. Gorman. v. 6, 1969–1970 (*The 20th Century: 1941–1970*). Pasadena, CA: Salem Press, 2008. 3288–3291.

Characterizes the "road to Woodstock" beginning with the 1967 Monterey International Pop Festival and the "road from Woodstock" leading to the Altamont Speedway concert. Breaks the essay into two sections: summary and significance. Describes the politically turbulent decade leading up to the festival and notes how the Woodstock Music and Art Fair "became a litmus test as to whether the counterculture could be true to its principles." Observes Woodstock, at the time, was a symbol of the power of the counterculture, suggesting the beginning of new order of "personal freedom, political pacifism, and social optimism." States history has shown it to have been the beginning of the end of the youth movement in America. Discusses the social conflicts within the counterculture, struggling between the youth movement as a political entity versus a lifestyle. Includes a short annotated bibliography.

195. Dalton, David. "Woodstock Planted Seeds of Activism that Persist Today." *Perspectives on Modern World History: Woodstock.* Ed. Louise I. Gerdes. Detroit, MI: Greenhaven Press, 2012. 94–101.

Suggests the Woodstock Music and Art Fair created a legacy that is still very present. Contains observations by individuals regarding the lasting impact of the event on their lives. Quotes from key persons, including comments from Michael Lang (co-founder of the festival), Michael Wadleigh (director of the motion picture *Woodstock*), Eddie Kramer (sound engineer), the author (former writer for *Rolling Stone* magazine), and festival performers Country Joe McDonald, Melanie, and Carlos Santana. Reports on several observations from these individuals claiming the event planted seeds of hope for a more peaceful world. Includes a sidebar of other historic events occurring in 1969, such as the Apollo moon landing, the Manson murders, and the disastrous Altamont Speedway concert featuring the Rolling Stones.

196. Doyle, Michael William. "The Woodstock Festival Site has Historical and Cultural Significance Worth Commemorating." *Perspectives on Modern World History: Woodstock.* Ed. Louise I. Gerdes. Detroit, MI: Greenhaven Press, 2012. 138–150.

> Excerpts from the *Preliminary Draft Generic Environmental Impact Statement of the Bethel Performing Arts Center,* on behalf of the Gerry Foundation (a corporation committed to building a museum at the original site of the festival). Outlines some of the ways in which the Woodstock Music and Art Fair has become ingrained in the cultural vocabulary and in American history. Offers the event was different from previous large-scale rock festivals because it featured the largest audience and selection of musicians ever assembled, lacked violence despite the presence of all the necessary conditions, and in many ways succeeded as it "took on the aspect of a high stakes experiment." Articulates the festival's symbolism, long-term significance, and impact on music (e.g., the advent of large-scale stadium concerts). Includes a sidebar on the band Santana.

197. "A Fleeting, Wonderful Moment of 'Community'." *Takin' it to the Streets: A Sixties Reader.* Eds. Alexander Bloom and Wini Breines. New York: Oxford University Press, 2003. 508–511.

> Reprints an article from *The New Yorker* published shortly after the Woodstock Music and Art Fair. Mentions one college student's experience attending the festival, noting he viewed the event much more positively than did the news media. Describes what it was like to be an attendee in terms of dealing with the traffic, obtaining food from The Hog Farm, and wandering the crowd. Notes the impact of the heavy rain storms and how audience members coped. Relays there was an overall air of good attitudes amongst the throngs.

198. Fong-Torres, Ben. "The Resurrection of Santana." *Not Fade Away: A Backstage Pass to 20 Years of Rock & Roll.* San Francisco, CA: Miller Freeman, 1999. 100–117. http://www.rollingstone.com/music/features/the-resurrection-of-santana-19721207

> Reprints a feature article on the group Santana originally appearing in *Rolling Stone* magazine (December 7, 1972). Quotes Bill Graham at length describing how he helped promote Santana and develop their career, including negotiating with Michael Lang to get the relatively unknown group a spot in the line-up for the Woodstock Music and Art Fair. Comments on his successful efforts to have Santana highlighted

in the motion picture *Woodstock*. Explains how Graham also managed to increase the group's payment for film rights by tenfold, from $750 to $7,500.

199. Frisch, Michael. "Woodstock and Altamont." *True Stories from the American Past*. Ed. William Graebner. New York: McGraw-Hill, 1993. 217–239.

Attempts to disjoin the Woodstock Music and Art Fair and the Altamont Speedway concert, two events from 1969 that evoke a good-vs-evil mythology convenient for capturing and summarizing the dichotomies of America in the 1960s. Describes how two investors (John Roberts and Joel Rosenman) entered into a partnership with two promoters (Michael Laing and Artie Kornfeld) to form Woodstock Ventures and plan the Woodstock festival. Explains how other key players came to be involved (e.g., Mel Lawrence, Chip Monck, Wes Pomeroy). Covers the failed attempt to stage the event in Walkill, New York, and the eventual site selection of Max Yasgur's farm near Bethel, New York. Points out the significance of Yasgur's support in launching the concert. Details the issues surrounding logistics, security, and the enlistment of the Hog Farm for assistance. Explores in detail the youth culture represented by Woodstock attendees and the influence of rock music in shaping the demographic. Recounts how the weekend unfolded in terms of the crowd size, the weather, and the use of illegal drugs. Contends this all somehow evolved into an idealized imagery in retrospect. Continues by reporting on the violence and murder at the Altamont Speedway concert held just a few months later. Concludes Woodstock "epitomized the values of culture, politics, and community at the core of generational change" and how these images can "transform the meaning of experience." Argues the Altamont Speedway concert, in reality, may have been more "innocent" than Woodstock in terms of the actual experience for the majority of attendees.

200. Frisch, Michael. "Woodstock Festival." *Encyclopedia of New York State*. Ed. Peter R. Eisenstadt. Syracuse, NY: Syracuse University Press, 2005. 1716–1717.

Describes the Woodstock Music and Fair from a somewhat historical context. Touches on the immediate aftermath and society's reactions and responses to the event. Observes the turmoil at the festival represented "free-form museum of urban problems." Claims "threat of chaos and the music-mediated response of strangers linked by self-discipline and collective self-help served to create a political, cultural, and musical generational community where none had quite existed." Notes the generational contrasts with both Woodstock '94 and Woodstock '99.

201. Glausser, Wayne. "Woodstock." *Cultural Encyclopedia of LSD.* Jefferson, NC: McFarland, 2011. 166–167.

Reports LSD was one of the more commonly used drugs at the Woodstock Music and Art Fair. Notes "widespread distribution and consumption of the drug went unchallenged by the police" at the festival. Explains how members of the Hog Farm preferred to talk someone off of a bad LSD trip as opposed to administering Thorazine. Observes the only significant drug casualty was a heroin-induced death. States LSD was a drug of choice at Woodstock '94 as well, but concerns were raised over the attendees' lack of experience with taking acid.

202. Graham, Bill, and Robert Greenfield. "Woodstock Nation." *Rock and Roll is here to Stay: An Anthology.* Ed. WIlliam McKeen. New York: W. W. Norton, 2000. 404–414.

Contains excerpts from an oral history project undertaken by the authors. Provides a perspective from Graham's Fillmore East crew who were drafted into helping organize the Woodstock Music and Art Fair. Includes comments by Graham and others on Graham's feelings towards the event. Carlos Santana describes how Graham coerced the promoters into putting the band Santana on the bill. Discusses the quality of performances and the poor conditions during the three days of the concert. Touches on the financial compensation of the musicians for both the event and the subsequent film. Includes quotes from Wavy Gravy, Carlos Santana, Pete Townshend, and several others involved with the festival.

203. Gravy, Wavy. "Hog Farming at Woodstock." *The Sixties: The Decade Remembered Now, by the People Who Lived it Then.* Ed. Lynda Rosen Obst. New York: Rolling Stone Press, 1977. 274–279.

Relays the experience of the Hog Farm being flown to and from the Woodstock Music and Art Fair and the author's impressions of working with festival attendees who were coping with bad drug trips. Explains the methodology employed by members of the Hog Farm to enlist volunteers in providing medical care and food services. Accompanied with large black and white photographs by Baron Wolman. Represents one chapter in a work of collected oral histories from individuals with unique perspectives on key events from the 1960s.

204. Hamilton, Neil A. "Woodstock." *The ABC-CLIO Companion to the 1960s Counterculture in America.* Santa Barbara, CA: ABC-CLIO, 1997. 336–338.

Focuses on the audience experience at the Woodstock Music and Art Fair more so than the music, noting the event was the personification of counterculture ideals. The publication as a whole elucidates in an encyclopedic format the people and events that challenged 1960s' society and made the period "among the most tumultuous, and controversial, in U.S. history."

205. Haskins, James, and Kathleen Benson. "The Music of the Sixties." *The 60s Reader.* New York: Viking Kestrel, 1988. 81–104.

Notes the first item to leave the shelves empty at Vassmer's General Store during the Woodstock Music and Art Fair was potato chips. Quotes the store's owners fifteen years after the event as noting not one of the checks cashed during the historic weekend bounced. Mentions the lingering general goodwill held regarding the festival, with many persons claiming to have been there who, in fact, were not in attendance. Observes Woodstock has come to symbolize the 1960s rather than the tragic Altamont Speedway concert where one audience member was murdered in front of the stage. Concludes this means overall positive aspects of the 1960s generation "struck a responsive chord."

206. Hertzberg, Hendrik. "You had to be there." *Politics: Observations and Arguments, 1966–2004.* New York: Penguin Press, 2004. 39–41.

Reprints an article from *The New Republic* (August 28, 1989) describing the author's personal account of having attended the Woodstock Music and Art Fair. Claims he went because of the rumor that Bob Dylan would be making an appearance at the festival. Describes journey to the site as a "vast medieval gypsy pilgrimage." Explains how he and his three friends managed in the mud and rain. Hertzberg is a political writer for *The New Yorker.*

207. "Jimi Hendrix's Post-Woodstock Comments." *Hendrix on Hendrix: Interviews and Encounters with Jimi Hendrix.* Ed. Steven Roby. Chicago: Chicago Review Press, 2012. 213.

Transcribes Jimi Hendrix's response to a reporter when asked to share his thoughts on the Woodstock Music and Art Fair that had just ended. Hendrix discusses nonviolence. From a Canadian radio broadcast (August 18, 1969).

208. Kirkpatrick, Rob. "Heaven in a Disaster Area." *1969: The Year Everything Changed.* New York: Skyhorse, 2009. 171–193.

Provides a detailed chronological narrative of the entire three days of the Woodstock Music and Art Fair and the trials, tribulations, missteps, and preparations leading up to it. Notes the event followed several months of numerous outdoor concerts, many featuring the same acts later to appear at Woodstock. These music festivals set the stage for increasingly large-scale, loosely-organized rock concerts. Describes the sets performed by each act at Woodstock. Envelops the entire narrative with the parallel tracking of Hurricane Camille. Touches on the legacy of the Woodstock festival.

209. Laure, Jason. "The Spontaneity of Woodstock Cannot be Reproduced." *Perspectives on Modern World History: Woodstock.* Ed. Louise I. Gerdes. Detroit, MI: Greenhaven Press, 2012. 167–170.

Suggests the "defining spontaneity" of the original Woodstock Music and Art Fair is elusive. Contends the event "grew to half a million by word of mouth alone" and there was no purpose other than to enjoy the music, a "common bond that transcended professional status, religion, education, and region." Claims the festival created community by allowing like-minded individuals to discover how many others shared their social perspectives.

210. Lerner, Steve. "Woodstock as a Coming-Out Party for Hippies." *Perspectives on Modern World History: Woodstock.* Ed. Louise I. Gerdes. Detroit, MI: Greenhaven Press, 2012. 58–66.

Reprints the author's *Village Voice* front page article from August 21, 1969. Describes the Woodstock Music and Art Fair in terms of being a pilgrimage to confirm the hippie lifestyle. Depicts the reactions of local residents as the onslaught of festival attendees began. Delves into the miserable drug-related conditions. Notes the event site was "like the Sinai Desert after the Egyptian retreat" as the crowds dispersed at the end of the festival, leaving shoes, sleeping bags, and other artifacts scattered across Max Yasgur's farm.

211. Madden, David W. "Woodstock Festival." *The Sixties in America.* Ed. Carl Singleton. Pasadena, CA: Salem Press, 1999. 793–795.

Recounts the origins, history, and basic key points of the Woodstock Music and Art Fair. Notes the promoters decided to have the performances run continuously so as to alleviate potential rioting due to the poor weather conditions and the unanticipated size of the crowd.

Concludes by commenting on the impact of the festival (e.g., growth of arena concerts, increased commercialism of rock music culture).

212. Marcus, Greil. "The Woodstock Festival." *20 Years of Rolling Stone: What a Long, Strange Trip it's Been.* Ed. Jann S. Wenner. New York: Friendly Press, 1987. 49–56.

Collects selected articles originally published in *Rolling Stone* during the magazine's first twenty years. Attempts to provide an "impressionistic chronology" suggesting a social and political history. Marcus relates his audience experience during the Woodstock Music and Art Fair, with particular attention given to the performance by Crosby, Stills, Nash & Young. Discusses the meaning of the event.

213. Moodie, David, and Maureen Callahan. "Don't Drink the Brown Water." *Da Capo: Best Music Writing 2000.* Ed. Peter Guralnick. New York: Da Capo Press, 2000. 72–97.

Recounts in great detail the behaviors of the crowds and promoters at Woodstock '99 leading to riots, rapes, and general mayhem. Describes the locale of the event as a former air base with "the surface of which was mostly concrete." Explains the extremely level site made it difficult for attendees to stay oriented. Discusses the commercialization and exploitation of the promoters and vendors, the poor sanitary conditions, and the attendees' experience of exceptional hot weather on a mostly concrete plateau. Suggests the audience was encouraged from the stage, by some of the performers, to act out violently. Highlights exceptionally aggressive assaults experienced by audience members in the mosh pits. Provides little commentary on the music.

214. Morrison, Joan, and Robert K. Morrison. "Bruce Hoffman." *From Camelot to Kent State: The Sixties Experience in the Words of those Who Lived it.* New York: Oxford University Press, 1987. 210–218.

Resides as a chapter in a book of oral histories on the 1960s. Hoffman spent his time at the Woodstock Music and Art Fair distributing thousands of cards printed with a picture of the Indian spiritual master Meher Baba. States he also helped attendees come off of bad drug trips.

215. Morrison, Joan, and Robert K. Morrison. "David Malcolm." *From Camelot to Kent State: The Sixties Experience in the Words of those Who Lived it.* New York: Oxford University Press, 1987. 202.

Resides as a chapter in a book of oral histories on the 1960s. Malcolm, now a newspaper editor, attended the Woodstock Music and Art Fair, but disliked most of it. Articulates distaste and hostility towards hippies and the 1960s counterculture. Believes the type of music played at the festival hasn't held up over time.

216. Morrison, Joan, and Robert K. Morrison. "Jason Zapator." *From Camelot to Kent State: The Sixties Experience in the Words of those Who Lived it.* New York: Oxford University Press, 1987. 197–201.

Resides as a chapter in a book of oral histories on the 1960s. Zapator was nineteen years old when he attended the Woodstock Music and Art Fair. Comments on his observations of the Hell's Angels, the Hog Farm, and the availability of illegal drugs. Describes performances by Melanie, The Who, and Jimi Hendrix.

217. Morrison, Joan, and Robert K. Morrison. "Kevin Compton." *From Camelot to Kent State: The Sixties Experience in the Words of those Who Lived it.* New York: Oxford University Press, 1987. 203–204.

Resides as a chapter in a book of oral histories on the 1960s. Compton attended the Woodstock Music and Art Fair while still in high school. Notes he was an outcast in his small hometown because of his long hair, but the large crowd at Woodstock showed him "how widespread the counterculture movement was." Acknowledges just because hippies all looked similar it didn't mean they shared the same values.

218. Morrison, Joan, and Robert K. Morrison. "Woodstock Nation." *The Rock History Reader.* Ed. Theo Cateforis. New York: Routledge, 2007. 115–119.

Acknowledges the Woodstock Music and Art Fair is mythologized "as the canonizing statement of the 1960s counterculture." Presents deviating recollections from three festival attendees. Illustrates the differing realities of the experience in order to refute popular myths regarding the concert as "a monolithic, unifying event." Draws from the authors' oral history project on the 1960s.

219. Onkey, Lauren. "Voodoo Child: Jimi Hendrix and the Politics of Race in the Sixties." *Imagine Nation: The American Counterculture of the 1960s and '70s.* Eds. Peter Braunstein and Michael William Doyle. New York: Routledge, 2001. 189–214. https://doi.org/10.4324/9780203615171

Compares and contrasts two Jimi Hendrix performances, held three weeks apart, to illustrate the politics of race in America during the 1960s. Suggests his set at the Woodstock Music and Art Fair, and the performance of *The Star Spangled Banner* in particular, became symbolic of the counterculture because the "crowd was struck dumb by this bravura deconstruction" of the national anthem by a "funkily elegant" dressed African-American who flashed a peace sign before starting to play. Notes Hendrix's performance later at the Harlem United Block Association benefit evoked a much different response. There, playing to a predominantly black audience mostly unfamiliar with his music, he was seen as being apart from the crowd, someone dissimilar. Continues by examining Hendrix's career as a "barometer of racial consciousness in the counterculture."

220. "Peace, Love and Mud." *1969: Woodstock, the Moon and Manson: The Turbulent End of the '60s.* Ed. Kelly Knauer. New York: Time Books, 2009. 84–87.

References The Museum at Bethel Woods, a structure dedicated to memorializing the Woodstock Music and Art Fair. Notes the topic of the festival was proven to still be controversial when the U.S. Senate defeated legislation that would have provided funding to help build the museum. Observes new technology makes the Woodstock experience more accessible than ever thanks to home movies and outtakes from the documentary film, *Woodstock* (available on YouTube at https://www.youtube.com/watch?v=czFr_kJCdKQ). Describes the festival as a "triumph of improvisation" when recounting the story of how the event barely happened and barely avoided disaster.

221. Potter, Sean. "The Impact of Weather on the Woodstock Festival." *Perspectives on Modern World History: Woodstock.* Ed. Louise I. Gerdes. Greenhaven Press: Greenhaven Press, 2012. 72–77.

Describes the significant impact of the weather leading up to and during the Woodstock Music and Art Fair. Claims heavy rains prior to the event made installing a fence around the site (in order to control access) difficult, thus making the event free to two-thirds of the attendees. States some performances ended early due to the weather. Observes by Sunday the festival site was "a sea of mud that was ankle-deep in some places." Discusses the audience's reaction to the weather and their collective coping strategies. Mentions the related effects of Hurricane Camille during this same weekend. Notes Woodstock '94 experienced similar conditions. The author is a meteorologist.

222. Rubin, Mike. "Summer of '69: Exploring the Cultural Battle between Charles Manson and Woodstock." *Spin Greatest Hits: 25 Years of Heretics, Heroes, and the New Rock 'n' Roll.* Ed. Doug Brod. Hoboken, NJ: John Wiley & sons, 2010. 28–44. http://www.spin.com/featured/charles-manson-woodstock-summer-of-69-spin-1994-cover-story/

Contrasts the Woodstock Music and Art Fair with the Manson Family murders, both events from August 1969. Acknowledges the Woodstock festival created briefly an euphoric endorsement for counterculture values of love and peace. Asserts, however, this was soon overshadowed by ongoing media coverage of the "sinister and pervasive" nature of Charles Manson and his followers. Points to the twenty-fifth anniversary music events celebrating the original Woodstock concert as evidence of its "monumental importance." Discusses Charles Manson as a "hippie doppelganger." Claims although antithetical, "Manson and Woodstock are inextricable linked, with Manson considered the Grim Reaper of the Woodstock dream." Suggests the current younger generation romanticizes Manson in order to express disappointment and exert rebellion against their parents' baby boom generation.

223. Shriver, Jerry. "Views on the Legacy of Woodstock Vary Significantly." *Perspectives on Modern World History: Woodstock.* Ed. Louise I. Gerdes. Detroit, MI: Greenhaven Press, 2012. 151–158.

Asserts the relevance of 1969's Woodstock Music and Art Fair varies substantially among individuals forty years after the event. Reports on "opinions expressed by festival attendees and participants, museum visitors, bloggers and readers queried by *USA Today*." Includes quotes from Paul Kantner (Jefferson Airplane), John Fogerty (Creedence Clearwater Revival), Dave Marsh (rock music critic), and Sam Yasgur (son of Max Yasgur), among others. Notes opinions regarding the festival range from it having been a paradise to an epic disaster, and from it representing youth united as a single voice to an accidental gathering without purpose. Concludes by stating the meaning of Woodstock is related to national identity because it was an exhibition of the freedom of expression.

224. Ward, Ed, Geoffrey Stokes, and Ken Tucker. "Woodstock... and Altamont." *Rock of Ages: The Rolling Stone History of Rock and Roll.* Harmondsworth, U.K.: Penguin Books, 1986. 420–446.

Begins with a description of the counterculture's social, political, and musical disparities, thus illustrating the lack of an actual singularity. Moves into a discussion on growth in the number of rock music festivals and their associated problems, such as violence. Delves into the Woodstock Music and Art Fair's economic appeal. Mentions the career successes of Santana and Joe Cocker spawned by the festival. Continues with an overview of major British recording artists of the time, including The Who, The Kinks, Led Zeppelin, and The Beatles. Concludes with a look at the Rolling Stones at the Altamont Speedway concert. Includes a list of the fees paid to many of the acts appearing at Woodstock.

225. Warner, Simon. "Reporting Woodstock: Some Contemporary Press Reflections on the Festival." *Remembering Woodstock.* Ed. Andy Bennett. Aldershot, U.K.: Ashgate, 2004. 55–74.

Studies how the print media, both mainstream and alternative presses, originally reported on the Woodstock Music and Art Fair. Attempts to "challenge the mythic status bestowed on the festival by subsequent memoirs." Asserts the festival "has been sold by a vocal generation who believed that the event was the apogee of their attainment." Reviews in depth the coverage provided at the time by the *New York Times*, *Village Voice*, and *Rolling Stone.* Includes a briefer section examining coverage by the British publications *The Guardian, Melody Maker,* and *New Musical Express.* Considers ideological stances of the publications and the related influences on the reporting. Includes a postscript in which two journalists (Greil Marcus and Tom Smucker) revisit and reflect on their original reporting.

Articles

226. Brady, John. "An Afternoon with Max Yasgur." *Popular Music and Society* 3 (1974): 24–40. https://doi.org/10.1080/03007767408591033

Describes the author's attempts and eventual success in interviewing Max Yasgur. Recounts first visiting Yasgur's farm, the location of the Woodstock Music and Art Fair, and an encounter with a young man making a pilgrimage to the site who recollected on having been at the festival. Relays observations of the event by three other individuals who also attended Woodstock. Shares stories of the ways in which area residents interacted with the festival attendees, including a local dentist who "let the kids come into his office and brush their teeth." Shares Yasgur's remarks regarding the festival, his generally favorable opinions on the counterculture generation, and the impact on his relationships with local citizens. Reports Yasgur received approximately 10,000 letters following the concert.

227. de Yampert, Rick. "Suffering from Entertainment Writers' Guilt no More." *Editor and Publisher* 127.40 (1994): 48, 33.

Recounts humorously the author's experience reporting on Woodstock '94. Describes being "issued second-class press credentials—ones which denied us access to the press tent with its precious phone lines and electrical outlets." Provides insight into the problems associated with reporting on such events.

228. Graves, Tom. "Peace, Love and Music." *American History* 30.6 (1996): 47+.

> Touches on all the key points related to staging the Woodstock Music and Art Fair. Mentions the planning for the festival, noting Michael Lang "had an almost mystical vision of the Woodstock festival." Comments on the traffic, security, and Abbie Hoffman's famous attempt to take the stage during the performance by The Who.

229. Howard, John A. "Principles in Default: Rediscovered and Reapplied." *Vital Speeches of the Day* 66.20 (2000): 618–619. http://www.stcroixreview.com/archives_nopass/2000-12/Howard.pdf

> Presents a speech by the conservative author delivered at the Annual Meeting of the Philadelphia Society in Chicago, Illinois (April 29, 2000). Cites quickly the author's attempt to stop the Woodstock Music and Art Fair upon learning of "the open use of marijuana and other illegal drugs." States he contacted the White House to urge the termination of the festival.

230. Isserman, Maurice. "3 Days of Peace and Music, 40 Years of Memory." *The Chronicle of Higher Education* 55.43 (2009): [n.p.].

> Reminisces on the author's own first-hand memories of the Woodstock Music and Art Fair and his "sense of having unexpectedly blundered into the opportunity to make history." Comments on the news media's prejudices against the event as it was unfolding. Uses Civil War commemorations as illustrative parallels to the Woodstock festival's enduring mythology of "innocence, self-reliance, and self-invention" owing much to the traditional American narrative. Acknowledges Woodstock was not an overtly political event, but also claims it would not have happened if it had not been for the Civil Rights movement and other political insurgencies of the 1960s. Observes the concert has also found its place in history as "a moment of reconciliation rather than confrontation." Suggests that the event should be remembered, like the Civil War, as a more complicated phenomenon.

231. Kopper, Philip. "Flashback to Woodstock." *American Heritage* 59.2 (2009): 14, 16. http://www.americanheritage.com/content/flashback-woodstock

> Describes the Bethel Woods Center for the Arts, a museum built to celebrate the Woodstock nation and the "zeitgeist that spawned it, and the phenomena that flowed from it." Uses the Woodstock Music and Art

Fair as a focal point, but the museum spans the Vietnam War, the Civil Rights Movement, and the counterculture.

232. Laure, Jason. "Memory of a Free Festival: Woodstock Thirty Years Later." *The World & I* 14.8 (1999): 233–239.

Offers first-person account of the Woodstock Music and Art Fair from a photographer who captured the event for the cover of *Newsweek*. Describes the event as "a watershed moment of American culture and a landmark of the twentieth century." Recalls being drawn to the event by the promise of music and with no plans on how to survive the weekend. States the music transcended social boundaries to create community. Claims efforts to recreate the spirit of the festival fail because the original spontaneity remains elusive.

233. McHugh, Catherine. "Mind Over Mud: How LD Allen Branton and Crew Brought 90s Technology Back to the Garden for Woodstock 94." *Lighting Dimensions* 18.8 (1994): 62–69, 165–174.

Details the process of creating and managing the lighting design for Woodstock '94. Offers insight into maintaining the lighting system in the face of adverse weather conditions. Delves into the problems associated with producing a large-scale event, including having to account for both natural daylight and nighttime performances. Notes the need to meet the lighting demands of the performers and set designers. Reproduces a drawing of the stage lighting plans. Includes a list of the lighting supervisory staff members and an itemization of the equipment used.

234. Noack, David. "Covering Woodstock." *Editor and Publisher* September 10 (1994): 16–18.

Describes how three daily newspapers covered Woodstock '94. Notes some of the planning that went into preparing to report from the site, the various logistics, and the associated problems in doing so that developed during the concert.

235. Parker, James. "Long Time Gone." *Atlantic Monthly* 304.2 (2009): 34–36. http://www.theatlantic.com/magazine/archive/2009/09/woodstock-nation/307611/

Reflects on the Woodstock Music and Art Fair for the 40th anniversary of the event. Considers through an examination of the motion picture *Woodstock* how and what has been encapsulated and portrayed for history versus what has been ignored or glossed over. Faults filmmaker Michael Wadleigh for not capturing some of the behind-the-scenes controversies, such as the Grateful Dead demanding cash payment up front. However, these are dismissed as "sideshows" that would only serve to distract from the overall narrative.

236. Sheehy, Michael. "Woodstock: How the Media Missed the Historic Angle of the Breaking Story." *Journalism History* 37.4 (2012): 238–246.

Explores why the iconic nature and cultural importance of the Woodstock Music and Art Fair was not initially realized, emphasized, or reported by major news media. Examines six daily newspapers (*New York Times, Washington Post, Wall Street Journal, Chicago Tribune, Los Angeles Times,* and *Cincinnati Enquirer*) and three magazines (*Time, Life,* and *Rolling Stone*) through the lens of framing theory to determine the prominence of the news event, the sources of information used to compile the coverage, and the extent to which the cultural aspects were given attention. Finds each publication used primarily official sources such as law enforcement representatives, as opposed to consulting actual attendees. As a result, the coverage focused mainly on the problems created by the festival rather than the broader social implications and significances. Suggests this "served the purpose of reinforcing the control of the ruling elites in society" despite Woodstock not being an intentionally political event.

237. Shipley, Morgan. "A Conversation with Wavy Gravy." *Journal for the Study of Radicalism* 6.2 (2012): 127–141. https://doi.org/10.1353/jsr.2012.0015

Transcribes an interview with Wavy Gravy (Hugh Romney), founder of the Hog Farm commune and participant in the Woodstock Music and Art Fair. Talks about many aspects of his life, such as his involvement with Acid Tests, his children's camp known as Camp Winnarainbow, his clown persona, philanthropic work, and the continuation of the Sixties ethos. Remarks on how he came to be involved with, and his experiences at, the Woodstock festival. Quotes him saying for the festival he "had a bear suit and a rubber shovel so if hippies built a stupid fire, I could burst out of the bushes and do my Smokey the Bear imitation." Mentions how the Hog Farm introduced the Woodstock audience to granola.

238. Sokol, David. "Down to Yasgur's Farm." *SEGDdesign*.22 (2008): 64–69. https://segd.org/museum-bethel-woods

Explains the creation of the Museum at Bethel Woods Center for the Arts, "an interpretive center on Yasgur's former fields dedicated to the cultural history of the 1960s and Woodstock." Describes the relationship between the museum and the associated performing arts center.

239. Spock, Daniel. "The Museum at Bethel Woods Center for the Arts: The Story of the Sixties and Woodstock." *Journal of American History* 97.1 (2010): 127–131. https://doi.org/10.2307/jahist/97.1.127

> Reviews in some detail the Museum at Bethel Woods Center for the Arts serving to memorialize the 1969 Woodstock Music and Art Fair. Reports on the politics behind the funding of the museum. Describes the exhibits, artifacts, and audiovisual presentations. Notes the museum reinforces existing notions of the event rather than attempting to overturn preconceptions. Asserts the Center "stands as a memorial more than a critical exercise." Questions the relevance of the place once the baby boom generation is no longer alive.

240. Yoders, Jeff. "Bronze Award: Back to the Garden." *Building Design & Construction* 48.5 (2007): 58–59. https://www.bdcnetwork.com/bronze-award-back-garden

> Describes the architecture of the Bethel Woods Center for the Arts near the historic site of the Woodstock Music and Art Fair. Delves into the origins of the museum including the purchase of the land by Alan Gerry and hiring of the architectural firm. Notes the New York State Office of Parks, Recreation, and Historic Preservation deemed the site of the original festival is of national significance and "asked that permanent construction not be placed within sight of the original natural amphitheater."

241. Zanetti, Mary. "Mathematical Lens: Woodstock Revisited." *The Mathematics Teacher* 103.4 (2009): 246–249.

> Uses both the Bethel Woods Center for the Arts, a performing arts venue and a museum dedicated to preserving the Woodstock Music and Art Fair experience, and data from the Woodstock festival itself to present mathematical exercises.

Websites

242. "A Clown for our Time." http://www.wavygravy.net/bio/biography.html

> Draws from what appears to be a website maintained by Wavy Gravy himself. Explains how The Hog Farm came to be at the Woodstock Music and Art Fair. Notes The Hog Farm was originally asked to "build fire pits and fire trails around the festival grounds" but convinced the promoters to allow them to set up a free kitchen as well. States they were later asked to serve as the festival's security. Describes experiencing an "amazing

energy that you could surrender to" at Woodstock which allowed The Hog Farm to operate at the event nonstop for the entire three days.

243. Lane, Steven. "A Conversation with an American Music Icon.... Arlo Guthrie." http://www.broowaha.com/articles/3344/a-conversation -with-an-american-music-icon-arlo-guthrie

From a 2008 interview, Arlo Guthrie describes what it was like to be at the Woodstock Music and Art Fair. Claims knowing at the time he was in a historic moment that was "wonderful and breathtakingly exhilarating." States he wishes he had been in a less altered state of mind since he was playing the biggest event in the history of music, but it still remains one of his fondest moments.

244. "'A Little Upstate Folk Festival': Woodstock and the Incredible String Band." http://www.makingtime.co.uk/beglad/woodstock.htm

Comments on the performance of the Incredible String Band at the Woodstock Music and Art Fair. Describes by what means the band came to play at the event and the manner of their arrival in a helicopter. Concentrates on how the band refused to go on stage due to the danger of playing electrical instruments in the heavy rain and was replaced by singer/songwriter Melanie (the band performed the next day). Notes later regrets about postponing their performance which resulted in the band not being included in the film nor on the record album. Suggests this affected negatively the group's career. States the Incredible String Band was possibly the only act at the Woodstock not to be called back for an encore. Mentions festival film footage of them performing *When You Find Out Who You Are* surfaced eventually.

245. McDonald, Joe. "Country Joe's Place: Woodstock 1969–1999." http://www.countryjoe.com/woodxxx.htm

This is a website created and maintained by Country Joe McDonald and devoted to all things "Woodstock." Includes the complete set lists for both the Country Joe McDonald and the Country Joe & The Fish performances at the 1969 festival.

246. McDonald, Joe. "County Joe's Place: Woodstock's 40th Anniversary." http://www.countryjoe.com/woodstock40.htm

This is a website created and maintained by Country Joe McDonald. Engages in a discourse on the accuracy of various sources proclaiming to present the correct performance order of artists at the Woodstock

Music and Art Fair. Includes postings from attendees offering their own versions of events.

247. Silas, Susan. "I Paid for Woodstock." http://www.corpse.org/index.php?option=com_content&task=view&id=787&Itemid=34

Provides a first-person account of attending the Woodstock Music and Art Fair. Describes the poor sanitation conditions and associated odors. Talks about how easy, yet unnecessary, it was to have people paged from the stage. Recalls Tim Hardin's apparently drug induced state and his being booed off the stage as a result. Comments on feeling urgency about attending the festival and after arriving then coming to realize the same sensation had been "felt by tens of thousands of other kids in big cities and small towns across the United States."

248. Stark, Jeff. "What a Riot: Diary of a Woodstock 99 Survivor." http://www.salon.com/1999/07/27/woodstock/

Offers a first-person diary of Woodstock '99. Describes the nearly hour-by-hour progression of deteriorating conditions and increasing unruliness of the crowd. Comments on many of the acts. Takes Fred Durst of Limp Bizkit to task for encouraging from the stage dangerous behavior among the audience in the pit.

249. Voice of America. "Singer-Songwriter Richie Havens Remembers His Woodstock." http://www.voanews.com/content/a-13-2009-08-15-voa7-68705132/409291.html

Focuses on the set performed by Richie Havens at the Woodstock Music and Art Fair. Describes the impromptu playing of *Freedom/Motherless Child* at the end of his three-hour performance. Havens observes although the festival was born out of the turbulence of the 1960s, the event itself was centered on "peace, love, and cheerfully dealing with the rain and mud." Notes Havens has continued to represent the Woodstock ethos throughout his career.

250. "Woodstock." http://www.woodstock.com

Seems to be an official Woodstock website. Contains videos (many of which appear to be from the motion picture *Woodstock*), photographs, and a news blog, all devoted to the Woodstock Music and Art Fair. Presents the entire chronological program of performers, their set lists, and brief commentaries on each act's experience at the festival. The website also sells Woodstock products (e.g., music, apparel, books, and other merchandise, including tote bags).

251. "Woodstock — Preservation archives." http://www.woodstock preservation.org/

> Represents the archives of the Woodstock Preservation Alliance, a group dedicated to perpetuating the spirit of the Woodstock Music and Art Fair and the preservation of the original site. Notes the group opposed the building of The Museum at Bethel Woods. Claims the original site is "a tangible reminder of the cultural, historical, and socially significant event that occurred there in 1969."

252. "Woodstock Music Festivals." http://topics.nytimes.com/top/reference/timestopics/subjects/w/woodstock_music_festivals/index.html

> *A New York Times* website updated continuously and dedicated to all things Woodstock. Links to more than 100 original articles from 1969 to present, including all Woodstock festivals to date. Contains videos and interactive media as well. Includes oral history videos submitted by readers. Points to other Woodstock-related websites as selected by the editors.

Transcriptions

253. "The Parable of the Hot Dogs at Woodstock." *Weekend Edition Saturday* (August 15, 2009). http://www.npr.org/2009/08/14/111898362/the-parable-of-the-hot-dogs-at-woodstock

> Commemorates the 40th anniversary of the Woodstock Music and Art Fair. Transcribes comments by Robert Goldstein (NPR music librarian and Woodstock attendee). Describes Goldstein's personal experience of surviving the event and his three hour quest for food to feed his friends and himself.

254. "Woodstock: We Went, We Saw, We Left." *All Things Considered* (August 14, 2009). http://www.npr.org/templates/story/story.php?story Id=111741353

> Transcribes Marcus Rosenbaum's recollections of his brief attendance at the Woodstock Music and Art Fair. Remarks "Woodstock was a blend of the miserable and the euphoric, the remarkable and the mundane, the sophisticated and the callow."

255. "Woodstock Memories, Mud and all." *All Things Considered* (August 14, 2009). http://www.npr.org/templates/story/story.php?story Id=111899515

> Presents interviews with key participants from the 1969 Woodstock Music and Art Fair, including Artie Kornfeld, Parry Teasdale, Michael Lang, Bill Thompson, Bob Solomon, and Richie Havens. Comments on the disorganization of the event and the festival's legacy.

256. "Woodstock Museum Re-Creates '69 Concert." *Weekend Edition Sunday* (July 27, 2008). http://www.npr.org/templates/story/story.php? storyId=92971931

> Transcribes interview of Michael Egan who is the Senior Director for The Museum at Bethel Woods, an institution located at the original site of the Woodstock Music and Art Fair and dedicated to remembering the 1960s. Discusses multimedia displays at the museum and the legacy of Woodstock. Includes snippets of commentary from persons associated with the festival. Ponders whether visitors to the museum contemplate the notion of the 1960s cultural revolution being reduced to "an exhibit, a little slice of history you can do in a couple of hours."

Videos

257. *The Creation of the Woodstock 1969 Music Festival: Birth of a Generation.* Dir. Donnelly, Patrick. Westlake Video, 1995.

> Presents the Woodstock Music and Art Fair from a historical perspective using interviews, film from the event, and photographs.

258. *Woodstock Diary.* Dir. Hegedus, Chris, Erez Laufer, and D. A. Pennebaker. Warner Bros. Pictures, 2009.

> Originally produced for television in 1994. Documents the 1969 Woodstock Arts and Music Fair. Contains footage of performances not seen in the original major theatrical film *Woodstock* (1970). Includes more contemporary interviews (*circa* 1994) with the festival producers and some of the participants, such as The Hog Farm's Wavy Gravy and Lisa Law.

Biography

Books

259. Baez, Joan. *And a Voice to Sing With: A Memoir*. New York: Summit Books, 1987.

Presents an autobiography account on the life of Joan Baez. Offers succinctly Baez's unique poetic impressions of the Woodstock Music and Art Fair. Describes sharing the helicopter ride to the site with her mother and Janis Joplin. Articulates Baez's humbled sense during the festival of belonging to the Woodstock generation. Compares the gathering to being like a city and a "technicolor, mud-splattered reflection of the 1960s."

260. Black, Johnny. *Jimi Hendrix: The Ultimate Experience*. New York: Thunder's Mouth Press, 1999.

Compiles, dissects, and arranges chronologically-by-event various interviews with numerous individuals to construct a diary-like biography of Jimi Hendrix. Quotes Eddie Kramer describing his discovery of how badly prepared things were at the Woodstock Music and Art Fair with regard to the technology utilized on stage. Mitch Mitchell mentions the poor conditions at the Holiday Inn used by Jimi Hendrix at the festival. Jerry Velez offers Woodstock was his first professional gig, but he didn't inform Hendrix of this fact. Leslie Aday reports Hendrix's drug-induced anxiety about going on stage at Woodstock and his post-performance disappointment. Jerry Morrison claims he was the one who encouraged Hendrix to play *The Star Spangled Banner* and Tom Law refers to Hendrix's rendition of the national anthem as being "a quintessential piece of art." Hendrix himself comments on the lack of attention to the sound equipment and his dismay for large rock music festivals. Larry Lee, Billy Cox, and Juma Sultan reflect upon the on-stage experience of playing with Hendrix at the event.

     http://dx.doi.org/10.11647/OBP.0105.03

261. Boyd, Joe. *White Bicycles: Making Music in the 1960s*. Serpent's Tale, 2006.

> Recollects episodes from the author's long and diverse career in the music business during the 1960s, when he worked with everyone from Muddy Waters to Pink Floyd before moving on to produce motion picture soundtrack albums. Relates his experience bringing the Incredible String Band to the Woodstock Music and Art Fair. Describes his regret over allowing the group to postpone their performance by one day due to the inclement weather, thus moving them out of the acoustic lineup (e.g., Joan Baez, John Sebastian) and into the middle of the more heavy electric bands (e.g., Canned Heat) where their set fell flat. Suggests the careers of the Incredible String Band members could have been transformed if they had played on Friday night at the festival, as originally planned.

262. Crosby, David, and Carl Gottlieb. *Long Time Gone: The Autobiography of David Crosby*. New York: Doubleday, 1988.

> Utilizes a variety of voices to create an unique autobiography of David Crosby. Reveals Crosby's generally positive feelings regarding the Woodstock Music and Art Fair. Explains Crosby, Stills, Nash & Young were "scared" when they took the stage because "the whole goddamn music business was standing in a circle behind us," noting everyone was curious about this new super-group. Quotes David Geffen describing his role in negotiating the inclusion of the group in the motion picture *Woodstock*.

263. Cross, Charles R. *Room Full of Mirrors: A Biography of Jimi Hendrix*. New York: Hyperion, 2005. https://www.scribd.com/doc/180427686/Room-Full-of-Mirrors-a-Biography-of-Jimi-Hendrix-Charles-R-Cross

> Presents a biography on the life of Jimi Hendrix. Notes Hendrix only rehearsed the band he used at the Woodstock Music and Art Fair for one week prior to the event. Tells the story of Hendrix and his band, along with Neil Young, needing to commandeer a truck in order to make it to the festival. Reprints Hendrix's introductory remarks from the festival's stage. Quotes Al Aronowitz describing the performance of *The Star Spangled Banner* as "the single greatest moment of the sixties." Mentions Hendrix's attitude toward his rendition of the national anthem as seeing it more of a musical exercise than a political manifesto. States the performance has become part of the Zeitgeist of the sixties. Reprints a poem Hendrix wrote about Woodstock.

264. Downing, David. *A Dreamer of Pictures: Neil Young the Man and His Music*. New York: Da Capo Press, 1994.

Explores Neil Young's life, politics, and aspirations. Mentions in a few words Young's ambivalence towards the Woodstock Music and Art Fair and notes he refused to be filmed at the festival during his performance with Crosby, Stills, Nash & Young. Includes a discography of record albums made by Neil Young as an individual artist and as part of a band from 1967 to 1993.

265. Echols, Alice. *Scars of Sweet Paradise: The Life and Times of Janis Joplin*. New York: Metropolitan Books, 1999.

Offers a biographical portrait of Janis Joplin. Relates Joplin's efforts to seek out a private place at the Woodstock Music and Art Fair in order to take illegal drugs. Describes her lackluster performance at the festival, attributing it mostly to drugs and alcohol.

266. Gelb, Arthur. *City Room*. New York: G. P. Putnam's Sons, 2003.

Represents the autobiography of Arthur Gelb, *New York Times* managing editor. Chronicles his forty-five year career at the newspaper. Describes how Gelb sent Barnard Collier to cover the Woodstock Music and Art Fair, thinking it was going to be just another music festival, along the lines of the Newport Folk Festivals. States, upon hearing reports of the massive traffic jam leading to Max Yasgur's farm, he assigned two more reporters to cover the festival. Comments on the specialized, all-access, treatment afforded exclusively to the trio of New *York Times* reporters, stating the promoters "fed them champagne and lobster." Also notes the wide-spread use of LSD at the festival. Reports on forming a post-event panel of attendees to discuss the significance of Woodstock, revealing the heightened sense of community where everything "was understood to be collective property." Claims the coverage provided by the newspaper crystalized and empowered the global counterculture community.

267. Glatt, John. *Rage & Roll: Bill Graham and the Selling of Rock*. New York: Birch Lane Press, 1993.

Offers a biography on rock music impresario Bill Graham (1931–1991). Provides insight into Graham's involvement with the Woodstock Music and Art Fair. Notes he was angered when the festival promoters started signing many of the acts scheduled to perform at his Fillmore East auditorium during the summer of 1969, fearing he would lose business if fans were able to see all the acts in one August weekend. States the solution agreed to by Michael Lang and Graham was to not announce the Woodstock acts until after they had played the Fillmore East during the summer. Claims John Morris hired many of the staff from the Fillmore East to work the Woodstock festival. Lists some of the fees paid to the acts. Describes how Graham negotiated getting Santana on the bill by threatening to withdraw the Grateful Dead. Quotes Graham discussing how Woodstock launched an era of stadium concerts and extraordinary fees being paid to performers. Observes this led directly to the demise of smaller concert venues such as the Fillmore East. Includes Graham's reaction to the motion picture *Woodstock* which includes a clip of Graham articulating criticism of the event.

268. Goldberg, Danny. *Bumping into Geniuses: My Life Inside the Rock and Roll Business*. New York: Gotham, 2008.

Presents the autobiography of Danny Goldberg, music industry insider. Describes Goldberg's experience as a concert reviewer for *Billboard* magazine assigned to the Woodstock Music and Art Fair. Confesses he has difficultly separating his memory of the festival from the images displayed in the motion picture *Woodstock*. Recalls the music as a backdrop to "the transient but ineffable sense of hippie camaraderie." Mentions being compelled by the performance of Santana to make his way to the front of the stage.

269. Graham, Bill, and Robert Greenfield. *Bill Graham Presents: My Life Inside Rock and Out*. New York: Doubleday, 1992.

Presents the autobiography of Bill Graham. Includes commentaries on Graham's involvement with the Woodstock Music and Art Fair. Covers his opposition to the festival, relationship with the promoters, and role in getting acts booked for the event. Quotes numerous individuals, including Graham, discussing his attendance and participation at Woodstock. Notes the festival organizers "capitalized on the smarts" of Fillmore East staff, including John Morris, Chip Monck, and Chris Langhart. Graham refers to the Woodstock promoters as "rank amateurs" who did not know what they were doing, but acknowledges no one had attempted anything of this scale before. Discusses how Graham managed to get Santana on the bill even though they had yet to release a record album. Includes Graham's negative comments on the event as excerpted from the motion picture *Woodstock*. Claims Martin Scorsese directed the filming of the festival more so than Michael Wadleigh because Scorsese was located at the front and center of the stage. Reports Graham stating his favorite performances at Woodstock were by The Who and Sly and the Family Stone. Graham also notes Jimi Hendrix's rendition of *The Star Spangled Banner* was "as creative a two minutes as you can probably find in rock and roll." Mentions Graham's observations on how Woodstock paved the way to a future of extremely large outdoor concerts.

270. Gravy, Wavy. *Something Good for a Change: Random Notes on Peace Thru Living*. New York: St. Martin's Press, 1992.

Recounts moments from the author's life. States the Hog Farm was originally hired for the Woodstock Music and Art Fair only to prepare the site (e.g., clear trails, dig fire pits), but when reporting for duty were informed they would be serving as security for the festival. Describes the Hog Farm's free kitchen at the event. Explains how the author came to be one of the persons giving the stage announcements. Fantasizes about a "Woodstock World" built on the site of the original festival 100 years after the event. Offers those at the concert "rose up to our highest common denominator and reflected it nationwide through the popular press." Expresses dismay the Woodstock generation ethos did not fully materialize in American culture, but remains hopeful for future generations.

271. Greenfield, Robert. *Dark Star: An Oral Biography of Jerry Garcia*. New York: William Morrow & Co., 1996.

Presents a series of short commentaries collected and arranged chronologically. Quotes Owsley Stanley and Nick Scully describing the Grateful Dead's performance at the Woodstock Music and Art Fair as a disaster due mostly to equipment problems.

272. Havens, Richie. *They Can't Hide Us Anymore*. New York: Avon Books, 1999.

Proclaims to not be an autobiography, but rather a book of impressions and experiences. Contains stories about Richie Havens and those persons who have affected his life. Begins with a description of Havens being ushered by helicopter to the Woodstock Music and Art Fair, and then shifts to recollections of his childhood. Returns to recalling the Woodstock festival, its eighteen foot high stage, and the sea of humanity. Describes how Havens came to be the first act to perform at the event as a result of Michael Lang begging him to get on stage since no other acts had arrived or were willing to go first. Shares his euphoric emotional state during the performance. Explains the spontaneity behind his final encore of *Freedom/Motherless Child*. Devotes some text to articulating the meaning behind Woodstock and the sacredness Havens feels for the location when he visits the site. Mentions various unsuccessful attempts to recreate the spirit of the event through anniversary concerts. Foreword by James Earl Jones.

273. Helm, Levon. *This Wheel's on Fire: Levon Helm and the Story of the Band.* Chicago: Chicago Review Press, 2013.

Recounts the author's life as a member of The Band. Describes how the group came to play at the Woodstock Music and Art Fair. States The Band felt as if they were going into a war zone based on what they had heard about the event from some of the first day's performers. Shares observations about the event. Lists the songs performed during The Band's set. Claims the group does not appear in the film or on the record album because of disputes over compensation. Notes also some disappointment with their set because Robbie Robertson's "microphone had been inadvertently left on, and he wasn't much of a singer."

274. Henderson, David. *The Life of Jimi Hendrix: 'Scuse Me while I Kiss the Sky.* London: Omnibus Press, 1990.

Provides an extensive biography of Jimi Hendrix. Mentions how Hendrix became the closing act of the Woodstock Music and Art Fair almost by default because, by this point in his career, no bands wanted to follow his sets. Breaks down his performance in some detail. Observes the final moments of Hendrix's performance were "both sad and beautiful, almost mournful yet exquisitely sculptured." Comments on the generally held disappointment with the sound recording of the festival, noting most of Hendrix's bandmates are essentially missing from the mix. This book is a newer edition of the author's *Jimi Hendrix: Voodoo Child of the Aquarian Age* (New York: Doubleday, 1978).

275. Jackson, Blair. *Garcia: An American Life.* New York: Penguin Books, 1999.

Offers the biography of Jerry Garcia. Describes Garcia's experiences at the Woodstock Music and Art Fair. Mentions how he wandered the festival's site under the influence of LSD. Contrasts the Woodstock performance by the Grateful Dead with the mythology of Woodstock where people helped each other survive the weekend and the music was "transcendent." Repeats the often reported self-criticism of the Grateful Dead's poor performance at the event. Suggests band members view their set in hindsight with both horror and glee, wearing their failure at such an historic event as a badge of honor. Quotes Garcia remarking on how everyone at Woodstock could sense the significance of the event as it was unfolding.

276. Kaliss, Jeff. *I Want to Take You Higher: The Life and Times of Sly & The Family Stone*. New York: Backbeat Books, 2008.

Presents a biography of Sly & the Family Stone, and Sylvester Stewart (Sly Stone) in particular. Points to the Woodstock Music and Art Fair as the group's monumental breakout event. Describes the festival experience from the perspective of the group's members. Their manager, David Kapralik, describes watching Sylvester Stewart perform as "Icarus, his wings made of wax, and [the spotlight] was the sun he flew too close to." Claims both the motion picture *Woodstock* and the sound recording, *Woodstock: Music from the Original Soundtrack and More,* gave a mythological status to the concert and the performers showcased within, including Sly & the Family Stone. Foreword by Sylvester Stewart. Preface by George Clinton. Includes a selected annotated discography.

277. Kennedy. *The Kennedy Chronicles: The Golden Age of MTV through Rose-Colored Glasses*. New York: Thomas Dunne, 2013.

Provides autobiographical account of Kennedy's years working for MTV as a VJ. Describes her experience covering Woodstock '94 for MTV. Relates her "all night journey" to discovery what was really happening at the festival after dark. Reports her shock, awe, and disgust at the public sodomy, excessive drug use, and lack of sanitation. Comments "the pungent fecal fragrance was warning strung out revelers to head for dryer ground." Mentions her brief flirtation with Dave Navarro, just prior to the Red Hot Chili Peppers taking the stage at the festival.

278. Keyser, Les. *Martin Scorsese*. New York: Twayne, 1992.

Presents a biography of Martin Scorsese, America's "most accomplished and most interesting filmmaker." Describes concisely Scorsese's involvement with making the motion picture *Woodstock*. Notes Scorsese spent his entire time at the Woodstock Music and Art Fair on the stage, filming the performances. Points out his arrival at the festival wearing expensive cufflinks as emblematic of the filmmaker's desire to be upper-class while simultaneously obsessing on the "dreams of outsiders and the music of iconoclasts and rebels." Includes a biographical chronology and a filmography.

279. Kindman, Michael "Mica". *My Odyssey through the Underground Press*. Ed. Ken Wachsberger. East Lansing, MI: Michigan State University Press, 2011.

> Conveys the author's life story and pivotal role in the development of the counterculture's underground press movement, from his 1963 enrollment at Michigan State University to his death from AIDS. Presents sketchily Kindman's experience at the Woodstock Music and Art Fair. Originally planning to use the opportunity to sell underground publications or, at least proselytize, he and his approximately twenty colleagues spent their entire time at the festival "directing traffic in the rain while one of the great cultural events of our generation went on around us." Reports they only heard the music dimly in the distance. Forewords by Paul Krassner and Tommi Avicolli Meca.

280. Kornfeld, Artie. *The Pied Piper of Woodstock*. Delray Beach, FL: Spirit of the Woodstock Nation, 2009.

> Presents the autobiography of Artie Kornfeld, one of the original four producers of the Woodstock Music and Art Fair. Shares extensively his life and the events that led him to help create the Woodstock festival. States the author was the youngest vice-president for Capitol Records at age twenty-one and had composed more than seventy-five songs that made it onto Billboard's charts. Devotes most of the book to Woodstock. Provides first-person account on the formation of Woodstock Ventures. Explains the evolution from the town of Woodstock, to Wallkill, and then on to Bethel with regard to deciding on and securing a site for the festival. Offers some background on the movie deal and other finances associated with the event. Offers commentary on every act that performed at Woodstock. Shares numerous personal incidents which occurred during the festival (e.g., a gun being pointed at the author's head). Reveals post-concert aftermaths. Contains photographs and reproductions of news clippings, as well as lyrics from Kornfeld's songs and paintings by Jim Warren.

281. Lang, Michael. *The Road to Woodstock*. New York: Ecco, 2009.

> Serves as a semi-autobiographical account of Michael Lang, one of the original promoters of the Woodstock Music and Art Fair. Provides the author's inside and unique perspective on the origin of the idea, planning of the event, and problems encountered along the way. Relies on extensive use of quotes from key individuals associated with the festival. Devotes chapters to each day of the concert and to the aftermath. Includes a "Where Are They Now" appendix and the complete set lists

of all the acts performing over the festival's three days. Includes some black and white photographs.

282. Langum, David J. *William M. Kunstler: The most Hated Lawyer in America*. New York: New York University Press, 1999.

Chronicles the career of William Kunstler, radical lawyer, director of the American Civil Liberties Union (ACLU), and defender of the Chicago Seven. Reveals Kunstler's attending the Woodstock Music and Art Fair at the invitation of Abbie Hoffman. Quotes Kunstler's description of a self-revelation experienced at the festival, which was his inability to identify with the youth of America.

283. Lesh, Phil. *Searching for the Sound: My Life with the Grateful Dead*. New York: Little, Brown, 2005.

Presents the autobiography of Phil Lesh, bass guitar player and founding member of The Grateful Dead. Contains a description of the band's experience at the Woodstock Music and Art Fair, including the endless waiting to perform and backstage incidents including a confrontation between Paul Kantner of Jefferson Airplane and Bill Graham. Discusses problems with the stage set-up, equipment, and electricity during their performance.

284. Marsh, Dave. *Before I Get Old: The Story of the Who*. New York: St. Martin's Press, 1983.

Offers a biography of The Who and a study on "the world in which the band lived and played." Chronicles from 1960 to 1980. Conveys the band's experience at the Woodstock Music and Art Fair. Notes the group did not share "the rhetoric of hippie pastoralism" so prevalent at the event. Reveals backstage machinations over paying the bands for their performances. Reports the frustrations The Who suffered over drug-spiked catering and the lengthy delay before they took the stage, some of which is used to explain the incidents of Pete Townshend kicking Michael Wadleigh and knocking Abbie Hoffman off the platform. Overall, the band members do not consider the performance at the festival to be one of their better sets.

285. McDermott, John. *Hendrix: Setting the Record Straight*. New York: Warner Books, 1992.

Presents a biography of Jimi Hendrix with a focus mostly on his years as a performer. Reports the conditions under which Hendrix agreed to perform at the Woodstock Music and Art Fair (i.e., he would be the headliner and close the festival as well as be the highest paid performer). Quotes Eddie Kramer commenting on the conditions for making sound recordings at the festival and the quality of Hendrix's set. Describes the backstage environment while Hendrix waited to take the stage. Suggests he may have been dosed unknowingly with illegal drugs shortly before his appearance. Recounts, song-by-song and in detail, Hendrix's uneven performance with a new under-rehearsed band. Notes Hendrix "repeatedly apologized" to the audience through his performance. Includes an annotated discography.

286. McDonough, Jimmy. *Shakey: Neil Young's Biography*. Random House, 2002.

Presents a detailed biography of Neil Young. Quotes Young commenting concisely on his performance at the Woodstock Music and Art Fair as a member of Crosby, Stills, Nash & Young. Quotes Young asserting the group was playing more to the cameras than to the audience and "Woodstock was a bullshit gig... we played fuckin' awful." Explains in his own words why he did not let himself be filmed for the motion picture *Woodstock*. Notes Young refused to play at Woodstock '94, despite a considerable financial offer to appear.

287. Mills, Randy K. *Troubled Hero: A Medal of Honor, Vietnam, and the War at Home*. Bloomington, IL: Indiana University Press, 2006.

Chronicles the story of Kenneth Kays, an anti-war college dropout who attended the Woodstock Music and Art Fair, was drafted into the Vietnam War, earned the Congressional Medal of Honor, and eventually took his own life after years of struggling with his involvement in the military. Notes how his plans to attend Woodstock almost didn't happen. Details his time at the concert with his traveling companions. Describes the impact of the festival as being both affirming and empowering. Suggests the event also contributed to his drug addictions. Continues by describing his life immediately after returning to his conservative hometown.

288. Reineke, Hank. *Arlo Guthrie: The Warner/Reprise Years*. Lanham, MD: Scarecrow Press, 2012.

Presents an unauthorized biography of Arlo Guthrie with particular attention to the years 1967 through 1981. Focuses on his professional career and musical output. Describes Guthrie's summer of 1969, his set at the Newport Folk Festival, and the events leading up to his appearance at the Woodstock Music and Art Fair (for which he was paid $5,000). Quotes Guthrie's immediate reflections on Woodstock including his observation that "it was probably one of the most wonderful moments of my life."

289. Roby, Steven. *Black Gold: The Lost Archives of Jimi Hendrix*. New York: Billboard Books, 2002.

Attempts to capture completely in text Jimi Hendrix's creativity in order to provide insights to his varied talents often overlooked. Discusses Hendrix's desire to be the closing act on Sunday night of the Woodstock Music and Art Fair and the amount of money he made from the performance and the film rights. Shares the disappointment he felt as Sunday night turned into Monday morning while waiting to perform at the festival. Discerns Hendrix's manager at the time wanted to control which songs Hendrix played at the concert. States how the auction of the guitar Hendrix played at Woodstock, a Fender Stratocaster, increased greatly the value of vintage guitars. Quotes Michael Wadleigh on the experience of filming Hendrix's Woodstock performance and the thrill of being physically close to him as he launched into *The Star Spangled Banner*. Includes a foreword by Noel Redding.

290. Rogan, Johnny. *Neil Young: Zero to Sixty*. London: Calidore Books, 2001.

Offers an extensive biography of Neil Young. States anticipated exposure of performing at the Woodstock Music and Art Fair was more important to Crosby, Stills, Nash & Young than the amount of money they would be paid ($5,000). Mentions Young's arrival at the event was by "truck and riding shotgun with Jimi Hendrix." Touches on the nervousness felt by the relatively new group playing at such a large event, "the most momentous gathering in the history of rock music," and in front of their peers. Notes the festival attendees were "forced to endure three days of hell." Observes Young's detachment during his performance and his refusal to be filmed during their set. Suggests in the long run this allowed him a certain amount of mystique and the ability to maintain a professional identity separate from the group. Discusses the record album *Woodstock: Music from the Original Soundtrack and More* and how Crosby, Stills, Nash & Young's vocal performances had been "doctored after the event." States the included recording of Young's song *Sea of Madness* was actually from a performance at the Fillmore East. Claims David Geffen would only allow footage of their set to be included in the motion picture *Woodstock* if their studio recordings of the songs *Long Time Gone* and *Woodstock* were used during the opening and closing credits. Asserts this helped elevated the group's legacy as the "living embodiment" of the Woodstock ethos. Includes a discography.

291. Rowes, Barbara. *Grace Slick: The Biography*. Garden City, NY: Doubleday, 1980.

Offers an authorized biography of Grace Slick. Explains how Jefferson Airplane learned of the plans for the Woodstock Music and Art Fair through Chip Monck. Describes Slick's experiences at the event, from swimming in the pool at the Holiday Inn where the acts were being housed to roaming the festival site with Paul Kantner prior to the start of the three-day concert. Notes Slick did not do much socializing, keeping to herself and not sharing her room with anyone. Relays the story of several of the managers representing the bands, including Jefferson Airplane's Bill Thompson, demanding their acts get paid prior to performing. States the start of Jefferson Airplane's set kept getting pushed back until it was nine hours later and in the early morning before they performed, after having spent the entire time sitting on the massive stage waiting their turn. Quotes Slick complaining about the lack of available bathroom facilities near backstage.

292. Selvin, Joel. *Sly and the Family Stone: An Oral History*. New York: Avon Books, 1998.

Represents a collection of commentaries by individuals who have worked with, known, or are related to Sylvester Stewart (Sly Stone). Quotes band member Larry Graham claiming the audience response while Sly and the Family Stone were on stage at the Woodstock Music and Art Fair made the group "rise to a level we had never been musically." Echoes Gregg Errico's description of the performer/audience energy-generating dynamic filling the air in the middle of the night during their set.

293. Shankar, Ravi. *Raga Mala: The Autobiography of Ravi Shankar*. New York: Welcome Rain Publishers, 1999.

Presents, in his own words, the life of Ravi Shankar. Mentions very briefly the author's experience at the Woodstock Music and Art Fair. Comments the audience reminded him "of the water buffalos you see in India, submerged in the mud." Reflects the music at the festival was incidental to the overall phenomenon. Regrets having played at the event because it was difficult to connect with the audience given the size and the widespread drug use. Claims there was, in fact, violence and sexual assaults at Woodstock and it was "not what people try to glorify it as today." Edited and introduced by George Harrison. Includes a glossary and a chronology.

294. Shapiro, Harry, and Caesar Glebbeek. *Jimi Hendrix: Electric Gypsy*. New York: St. Martin's Press, 1990.

Presents a biographical account on the life of Jimi Hendrix. Describes the disorganization surrounding the Woodstock Music and Art Fair and the resulting reluctance of Hendrix to honor his commitment. States Hendrix's performance at the festival was "loose and sprawling" mixed with "some very fine moments" of solo improvisations. Discusses his rendition of *The Star Spangled Banner,* noting the performance sent shock waves throughout the audience. Delves into Hendrix's political leanings, suggesting he had a fatalistic viewpoint which influenced his set in front of thousands of comfortably middle-class white Americans. Includes an extensive discography with notes, a technical file describing the instruments and equipment used by Hendrix throughout his career, a lengthy chronology of key events, the Hendrix family tree, and a bibliography/filmography.

295. Shapiro, Marc. *Carlos Santana: Back on Top*. New York: St. Martin's Press, 2000.

Presents a biography of Carlos Santana. Tells the story of how Bill Graham managed to get Santana booked to play the Woodstock Music and Art Fair even though they were not well known and had not yet released their first album. Mentions Carlos Santana's excitement and fear of playing before such a large audience. States Carlos Santana took the stage in a drug-induced haze which increased his fear. Claims he doesn't remember much of the set until the end when they started to play *Soul Sacrifice*. Includes a discography.

296. Sheehy, Gail. *Daring: My Passages*. New York: HarperCollins, 2014.

Presents an autobiography of author Gail Sheeny. Includes a brief description of her trip to the Woodstock Music and Art Fair with her sister and a friend. Claims they were the only attendees not high on drugs. States the festival brought her and her sister closer together.

297. Sloman, Larry. *Steal this Dream: Abbie Hoffman and the Countercultural Revolution in America*. New York: Doubleday, 1998.

Offers a biography on Abbie Hoffman using excerpted quotes from individuals associated with him throughout his life. Describes Hoffman's attempts to shape the Woodstock Music and Art Fair as early as the planning stages and his efforts to extract $65,000 from the promoters. Shares stories from the festival about how Hoffman and his associates interacted with the event's staff and the filmmakers. Provides an alternative version of how Hoffman came to be knocked of the stage by Pete Townshend during the performance by The Who. Claims there was a misunderstanding between Hoffman and The Who regarding whether Hoffman had three minutes to make a political statement from the stage. Foreword by Howard Stern. Includes a "Where are They Now?" section.

298. Sounes, Howard. *Down the Highway: The Life of Bob Dylan*. New York: Grove Press, 2001.

Constructs a discerning biography of Bob Dylan built extensively on interviews with more than 250 individuals. States sketchily the impact of the Woodstock Music and Art Fair on the town of Woodstock, New York, some sixty miles from the concert. Quotes Bob Dylan's disparaging remarks about the festival. Provides some insight into Dylan's performance at Woodstock '94, suggesting he showed a lack of confidence before taking the stage, but the reaction to his performance indicated "his music had transcended its time." Claims Dylan was paid $600,000 to appear at the 1994 event.

299. Taylor, Dallas. *Prisoner of Woodstock*. New York: Thunder's Mouth Press, 1994.

Presents the author's autobiography as a Los Angeles-based musician and drummer for Crosby, Stills, Nash & Young. Describes the aerial view and first impressions of arriving to the Woodstock Music and Art Fair in a helicopter. Provides a detailed personalized account of the festival from both a backstage and onstage perspective. Discusses his drug induced anxieties about the event. Introductions by David Crosby and Graham Nash.

300. Tiber, Elliot. *Knock on Woodstock: The Uproarious, Uncensored Story of the Woodstock Festival, the Gay Man Who made it Happen, and how He Earned His Ticket to Freedom*. New York: Festival Books, 1994.

Publishes the author's first of three books to date on the Woodstock Music and Art Fair. Intends to be a humorous and satirical account of Tiber's role in helping the event come into existence. Includes the disclaimer "that fact and fiction, according to the absurd, twisted, world of the author, are often unclear and any offence or implied derogatory statements about any person, living, dead, or in suspended animation, is purely coincidental." Foreword by Richie Havens.

301. Tiber, Elliot. *Taking Woodstock*. Garden City Park, NY: Square One, 2007.

Describes the author's efforts to save his family's motel and consequently his participation in placing the Woodstock Music and Art Fair on Max Yasgur's farm. Tells the story through the lens of Tiber's homosexuality. Includes an epilogue, bringing his life and the events of the book up to the present. Dedicated to Michael Lang and Andre Ernotte. This memoir was made into a motion picture, *Taking Woodstock* (2009), directed by Ang Lee.

302. Weinstein, Norman. *Carlos Santana: A Biography*. Santa Barbara, CA: Greenwood Press, 2009.

Discusses the instrumental role Bill Graham played in getting Santana onto the stage at the Woodstock Music and Art Fair despite the band not being known outside of the San Francisco area. Comments on the way in which the motion picture *Woodstock* captured the "highpoint of the band's shining debut" in their performance of *Soul Sacrifice*. Reveals the monumental influence of the performance on Carlos Santana's career and his acknowledgement of it. Includes a selected discography.

303. Weller, Sheila. *Girls Like Us: Carole King, Joni Mitchell, Carly Simon — and the Journey of a Generation*. New York: Atria, 2008.

Examines the careers of Carole King, Joni Mitchell, and Carly Simon. Explains why Joni Mitchell did not perform at the Woodstock Music and Art Fair although she was touring at the time with Crosby, Stills & Nash. Provides an overview of the festival and Mitchell's perspective. Describes how she came to write the song *Woodstock*.

304. Yasgur, Sam. *Max B. Yasgur: The Woodstock Festival's Famous Farmer*. Woodbury, NY: Katrina Woodstock, 2009.

Presents an admittedly subjective biography of Max Yasgur, the farmer who leased his land for the 1969 Woodstock Music and Art Fair, written by Max's son. Reconstructs from memory the life of Max Yasgur and, in particular, his introduction and involvement with the festival. Desires to clarify "misleading statements, the half-truths, and the made up junk" and to circumvent those who would use the Yasgur name to profit on the

Woodstock festival. Observes Max had little in common with Woodstock attendees, including politics, music, and culture, but he did hold a strong belief in their right to express themselves. Suggests his life may have been shortened as a result of Woodstock.

305. Zimmer, Dave. *Crosby, Stills, & Nash: The Authorized Biography.* New York: Da Capo Press, 2000.

Chronicles the history of Crosby, Stills & Nash. Claims no other group performing at the Woodstock Music and Art Fair represented the cultural ethos of the time more than Crosby, Stills, Nash & Young. Mentions how Joni Mitchell, who was touring with the band at the time, was denied the opportunity to perform at the festival. States famous self-proclaimed remark from the stage about the group being "scared shitless" was about the scrutiny of all the music industry personnel watching them perform from immediately off stage. Notes Neil Young's refusal to be filmed during the event. Quotes Joni Mitchell describing her motivation for writing the song *Woodstock*. Includes a foreword by Graham Nash and a discography.

Chapters

306. Glausser, Wayne. "Wavy Gravy." *Cultural Encyclopedia of LSD.* Jefferson, NC: McFarland, 2011. 163.

Summarizes in brief the biography of Wavy Gravy. Notes Wavy Gravy referred to his security team at the Woodstock Music and Art Fair as the "Please Force."

307. Kisseloff, Jeff. "Barry Melton: The Guitarist." *Generation on Fire: Voices of Protest from the 1960s.* Lexington, KY: University Press of Kentucky, 2006. 194–209.

Continues the author's work in the field of oral history. Profiles "those Americans who stood up and said no to war, greed, racism, sexism, homophobia, pollution, censorship, lame music, and bad haircuts." Serves as a biographical profile of Barry Melton. Provides a brief first person account of the Country Joe & the Fish performance at the Woodstock Music and Art Fair from an on-stage perspective. Offers personal insight into a range of the late 1960s counterculture events, personalities, and experiences.

308. McDonald, Country Joe, and Dave Allen. "Afterword: Country Joe McDonald Remembering Woodstock." *Remembering Woodstock.* Ed. Andy Bennett. Aldershot, U.K.: Ashgate, 2004. 146–153.

Uses the Woodstock Music and Art Fair as a life-altering milestone to provide a brief autobiographical account on the life of Country Joe McDonald leading up to the festival, during the event itself, and living with the resulting post-event effects. Reflects on the impact of the Vietnam War on his generation. Includes a discography.

Music

Books

309. Boyd, Todd. *The New H.N.I.C. (Head Niggas in Charge): The Death of Civil Rights and the Reign of Hip Hop.* New York: New York University Press, 2002.

> Discusses, in part, the use of the word "nigger" and "nigga" in hip-hop context. Mentions the DMX performance at Woodstock '99 with a call-and-response with, in this case, a mostly white audience. Offers Woodstock '99 and the motion picture *Any Given Sunday* as two examples in which these words of "endearment are used in ways other than to affirm a strong sense of Black unity." Claims hip-hop music at its core is "this battle over language and representation." Includes a glossary of hip-hop terms.

310. Floyd, Samuel A. *The Power of Black Music: Interpreting its History from Africa to the United States.* New York: Oxford University Press, 1995.

> Cites Jimi Hendrix's interpretation of *The Star Spangled Banner* at the Woodstock Music and Art Fair as an example of his execution style coming from the "practice and proclivities of numerous ancient and modern African and African-American music makers." Declares the performance to be an important event in the history of American music. Notes the way in which Hendrix comments on the topic of the song using just his guitar playing without singing the lyrics.

311. Garofalo, Reebee. *Rockin' Out: Popular Music in the USA.* Upper Saddle River, NJ: Prentice Hall, 2011.

> Serves as a textbook concentrating on the relationship between popular music and mass culture. Asserts popular music is "a social and political

     http://dx.doi.org/10.11647/OBP.0105.04

indicator that mirrors and influences the society in which we live." Notes the 1969 Woodstock Music and Art Fair offered "a fleeting pastoral approximation" of the overall counterculture utopian vision. Touches briefly on Woodstock '94 and Woodstock '99 mainly to provide and discuss stark contrasts to the 1969 event.

312. Hopkins, Jerry, Jim Marshall, and Baron Wolman. *Festival: The Book of American Music Celebrations.* New York: Macmillan, 1970.

Combines reprints of articles and sections of books with numerous black and white photographs to create a single narrative on American music festivals. Includes bluegrass, rock, and folk festivals held in the 1960s. In particular, notes that at the Woodstock Music and Art Fair there was "forged a new definition of performance, wherein the performers and audience are one and all normal barriers are removed."

313. Jennings, Nicholas. *Before the Gold Rush: Flashbacks to the Dawn of the Canadian Sound.* Toronto, Canada: Viking, 1997.

Offers a history of Canadian music in the 1960s, where "bands existed in their home towns on the strength of their fan clubs and word-of-mouth reputations." Mentions in brief the Canadian musicians who performed at the Woodstock Music and Art Fair (Neil Young, David Clayton-Thomas of Blood, Sweat & Tears, and members of The Band). Quotes Clayton-Thomas explaining how the festival was not the best venue for communicating the subtleties of his group's music. Notes by having performed at an event that took on mythical importance, Blood, Sweat & Tears experienced a surge in popularity as a touring act.

314. McMichael, Joe, and Jack Lyons. *The Who Concert File.* London: Omnibus Press, 1997.

Documents every performance by The Who; sometimes including specific venues, set lists, and commentaries. Remarks on the overall negative experience for the band of the Woodstock Music and Art Fair. Mentions particularly strong performances of some songs during their set. Recounts Peter Townshend hitting Abbie Hoffman over the head with a guitar during the show. Contains numerous photographs of the group and memorabilia, such as concert posters and tickets. Foreword by Peter Townshend.

315. Murray, Charles Shaar. *Crosstown Traffic: Jimi Hendrix and the Post-War Rock 'n' Roll Revolution.* New York: St. Martin's Press, 1989.

Explores the life of, and world around, Jimi Hendrix through an examination of his music. Claims Hendrix's performance at the

Woodstock Music and Art Fair as captured in the motion picture *Woodstock* "defined what Woodstock was about for the rest of the world." Declares his rendition of *The Star Spangled Banner* was epic, comparing Hendrix to John Coltrane and describing the performance as "a compelling musical allegory of a nation tearing itself apart." Provides a description of the allegorical references.

316. Myers, Marc. *Why Jazz Happened*. Berkeley, CA: University of California Press, 2013.

Presents an extensive history of jazz music, including all of the social forces that have driven its evolution. Delves into the impact of electronic music and the influences of the sound and lighting systems that emerged with the advent of large outdoor concerts and music festivals. Details Bill Hanley's role in designing the sound system used at the Woodstock Music and Art Fair. Articulates the thinking behind the massive towers that held the speaker system and the last-minute changes required to accommodate a much larger than expected audience, such as needing to boost the sound levels without creating distortion. Notes a change in audience attitudes toward music as a result of the extended performances at Woodstock. Suggests attendees came to believe "longer songs and solos were musical extensions of their own rebellions and anxieties." Contends all of this influenced greatly the presentation of jazz music.

317. Pollock, Bruce. *By the Time We Got to Woodstock: The Great Rock 'n' Roll Revolution of 1969*. New York: Backbeat Books, 2009.

Proclaims 1969 to have been "a year of radical and profound personal risks, changes, and choices in the way music was perceived, written about, experienced, exploited, played, and disseminated." Scatters throughout the text first-hand accounts of the Woodstock Music and Art Fair from musicians who performed at the festival. Includes interview quotes from Richie Havens and John Sebastian discussing their performances at the event.

318. Santelli, Robert. *Sixties: A Listener's Guide*. Chicago: Contemporary Books, 1985.

Includes an "overview of every major rock category that figured prominently in the sixties" as well as brief biographies of selected musicians. Notes whether a performer appeared at the Woodstock Music and Art Fair. Claims the performance at the festival of *I'm Going Home* by the group Ten Years After "may be the fastest rock guitar solo recorded in the sixties." Includes the author's choices for the top twenty-five albums of the decade.

319. Unterberger, Richie. *Eight Miles High: Folk-Rock's Flight from Haight-Ashbury to Woodstock.* San Francisco, CA: Backbeat Books, 2003.

> Highlights the evolution of folk-rock music in the latter half of the 1960s. Observes folk-rock musicians at the Woodstock Music and Art Fair held their own against big rock acts, such as The Who and Jimi Hendrix. Explores the openness of the counterculture to folk music. Describes acoustic and semi-acoustic performances by Richie Havens, Country Joe McDonald, John Sebastian, Tim Hardin, Melanie, Arlo Guthrie, the Incredible String Band, and Crosby, Stills Nash & Young. Also references Woodstock performances that were born from the folk tradition, including the sets by Jefferson Airplane and Ten Years After. Includes an annotated discography.

Chapters

320. Allen, Dave. "A Public Transition: Acoustic and Electric Performances at the Woodstock Festival." *Remembering Woodstock.* Ed. Andy Bennett. Aldershot, U.K.: Ashgate, 2004. 111–126.

> Argues both acoustic (rural) and electric (urban) music lived equally within the context of popular music during the 1960s, up to the Woodstock Music and Art Fair which was "almost the last very public celebration of the rural within popular music" and the last occasion where acoustic and electric acts shared the stage equally. Notes Country Joe McDonald performed twice at the festival, once as a solo acoustic act and once with his electric rock band. Illustrates the premise using McDonald's performances (as represented in the motion picture *Woodstock*) and their subsequent impact on his career. Provides a brief history of McDonald's evolution as a musician, from acoustic to electric. Questions whether acoustic music still has any significance in contemporary popular music.

321. Bordowitz, Hank. "From Monterey Pop to Woodstock to Altamont: Innocence Found and Lost." *Turning Points in Rock and Roll: The Key Events that Affected Popular Music in the Latter Half of the 20th Century.* New York: Citadel Press, 2004. 155–171.

> Traces the history of large-scale rock festivals from the charming Monterey International Pop Festival in 1967 through the counterculture's utopian Woodstock Music and Art Fair to the violence of the Altamont Speedway concert, the latter two both held in 1969. Claims the Woodstock festival was "the highwater mark of the rising tide of utopian spirit started at Monterey." Notes the decline of such ambitious concerts in America that followed and the rise of the same in Europe. Continues by discussing

the traveling caravan Lollapalooza and the Lilith Fair tours that emerged in the 1990s. Explores an underline theme of the evolving relationship between art and commerce.

322. Clarke, Eric F. "Jimi Hendrix's 'Star Spangled Banner'." *Ways of Listening: An Ecological Approach to the Perception of Musical Meaning.* Oxford, U.K.: Oxford University Press, 2005. 48–61. https://doi.org/10.1093/acprof:oso/9780195151947.003.0003

Asserts Jimi Hendrix's performance of *The Star Spangled Banner* at the Woodstock Music and Art Fair articulates a history-making musical protest of the Vietnam War. Traces the impact of the sounds themselves, as opposed to the circumstances of the delivery and/or the political projections of those interpreting the meaning of the event. Draws an analysis from the sound recording so as not to be influenced by the imagery in the motion picture *Woodstock*. Continues with a second-by-second breakdown of the performance, describing musical notes and how they are rendered throughout the performance. Highlights Hendrix's insertion of "Taps" (a bugle call played at dusk, during flag ceremonies, and at military funerals by the United States armed forces) into the national anthem. Claims nationalism and counterculture are both "simultaneously and antagonistically specified in the sounds of the performance." Includes a transcription musical score of Hendrix's performance of *The Star Spangled Banner*.

323. Daley, Mike. "Land of the Free: Jimi Hendrix—Woodstock Festival, August 18, 1969." *Performance and Popular Music: History, Place and Time.* Ed. Ian Inglis. Aldershot, U.K.: Ashgate, 2006. 52–57.

Recounts in detail Jimi Hendrix's set at the Woodstock Music and Art Fair. Observes Hendrix's performance has come to fully represent the Woodstock festival "as a cultural signpost in rock history." Argues the significance of Hendrix's appearance at the concert has been a relatively recent development and not evident in the press immediately following the event. Provides insight into Hendrix's preparations for the festival, including his desire to take his music in a new direction and the associated auditioning of new musicians. Describes the actual performance as "loose and somewhat confused." Delves into a moment by moment description of Hendrix's rendering of *The Star Spangled Banner*. Claims his presentation of the national anthem revealed a "more conflicted view of the war in Vietnam than would be suggested by many of those who have offered interpretations." Claims Hendrix's appearance at Woodstock symbolizes both the free-spirit of the 1960s and the "troubled heart of the anti-war movement."

324. Fast, Susan, and Kip Pegley. "Introduction." *Music, Politics, and Violence.* Eds. Susan Fast and Kip Pegley. Middletown, CT: Wesleyan University Press, 2012. 1–33.

> Reveals how music and violence entwine. Suggests music is a "rich medium for perpetuating symbolic violence, which, in turn, often becomes part of a much larger systemic oppression." Questions what can be learned about intentionality of a "translation's transformative power to prompt political change" when examining lyrics and music. Points to Jimi Hendrix's rendition of *The Star Spangled Banner* at the Woodstock Music and Art Fair as a prime example. Observes in Hendrix's performance a "use of extreme distortion and feedback wreaking timbral havoc on the melody" and, thus, framing the national anthem in a new way. Suggests Hendrix transformed the song from celebratory to protest by virtue of digressing from the melody, inserting feedback, incorporating *Taps*, and conjuring a feeling of chaos and violence. Debates Hendrix's exact intentions behind such an interpretation by offering conflicting evidence. Concludes that regardless of intent, one may hear the performance "informed by a Zeitgeist and part of a larger critique of American involvement in the Vietnam War." Claims this is but one example of how music is used to "articulate notions of otherness."

325. Hicks, Bob. "Jimi Hendrix: A Memorial (Northwest Passage, 29th September 1970)." *The Jimi Hendrix Companion: Three Decades of Commentary.* Ed. Chris Potash. New York: Schirmer, 1996. 207–210.

> Compiles previously published articles about Jimi Hendrix. In an item published shortly after Hendrix's death from *Northwest Passage*, an underground newspaper, Hicks comments on Hendrix's performance at the Woodstock Music and Art Fair. Claims Hendrix reached the height of his artistic maturity at the festival. Describes Hendrix's set as "a vision of cultural crisis, of structural breakdown and chaos." Observes his performance of *The Star Spangled Banner* was "the vast underbelly of a culture sinking." Questions whether the audience understood the meaning of the performance.

326. Jopling, Norman. "Man, Myth or Magic? Jimi Hendrix is Back, and Happy, and Talking..." *Hendrix on Hendrix: Interviews and Encounters with Jimi Hendrix.* Ed. Steven Roby. Chicago: Chicago Review Press, 2012. 289–292.

> Transcribes interview with Jimi Hendrix from September 12, 1970 in which he mentions his favorite performances from the Woodstock

Music and Art Fair (i.e., Sly and the Family Stone, Rickie Havens, and Ten Years After).

327. Nunez, Sigrid. "Woodstock at Max Yasgur's Farm: Bethel, New York, August 15–17, 1969." *The Show I'll Never Forget: 50 Writers Relive their most Memorable Concertgoing Experience.* Ed. Sean Manning. Cambridge, MA: Da Capo Press, 2007. 52–57.

> Relates the author's experience attending, and thoughts regarding, the Woodstock Music and Art Fair. Asserts she "went to Woodstock on the back of a motorcycle driven by a Vietnam vet who was on acid." Describes how unprepared she was for the weather, the crowd, and lack of food. Recounts the amount of drug use among her traveling companions. Comments on her favorite performers (e.g., Janis Joplin, Sly and the Family Stone), but acknowledges that for years she remembered the performance of Ten Years After only to realize much later they performed after she had left. Attributes this to having seen the band play in the motion picture *Woodstock*. States initially it was a notable distinction among peers to have been at the festival, but it has now come to mainly remind her of her progressing age.

328. Perone, James E. "Woodstock: Music from the Original Soundtrack and More (1970)." *The Album: A Guide to Pop Music's most Provocative, Influential, and Important Creations.* Ed. James E. Perone. Santa Barbara, CA: Praeger, 2012.

> Critiques track-by-track the sound recording *Woodstock: Music from the Original Soundtrack and More*, released in 1970 and loosely served as the soundtrack album to motion picture *Woodstock*. Notes although some of the acts featured on the recording are not shown in the film, the album represents "one of the most important live albums of the rock era." Comments on the re-sequencing of performances away from the actual chronology of events. Offers the record's producer, Eric Blackstead, did this as well as adding stage announcements and crowd noise in order to convey to the listener the emotional experience of the festival. Includes a brief sidebar on rock music festivals of the 1960s.

329. Sullivan, Denise. "Rainbow Politics, Woodstock, and Revolution Rock." *Keep on Pushing: Black Power Music from Blues to Hip-Hop.* Chicago: Lawrence Hill Books, 2011. 99–108.

> Bookends an essay on the significance of the Woodstock Music and Art Fair to the black experience with thoughts on Richie Havens and Jimi

Hendrix. Provides Haven's perspective on the festival and its relationship to his life. Notes his performance at the event was so dynamic as to allow him to sustain a lifelong career as a performer. Alternatively, Hendrix's showing at the event suggested a beginning of the end. Discusses Hendrix's relationship with both black and white audiences. Suggests "Jimi Hendrix was a freedom rider" despite his apolitical image. Notes that performers of color (Richie Havens, Jimi Hendrix, Sly Stone, Carlos Santana) triumphed at Woodstock. Claims Santana's performance "was in essence the moment that birthed the Latino rock movement."

330. "United Block Association Press Conference." *Hendrix on Hendrix: Interviews and Encounters with Jimi Hendrix.* Ed. Steven Roby. Chicago: Chicago Review Press, 2012. 215–218.

Transcribes a Jimi Hendrix press conference from August 1969 held to promote an upcoming benefit concert for Harlem's United Block Association. Hendrix comments on the Woodstock Music and Art Fair, including his performance of *The Star Spangled Banner*, the wide spread drug use and lack of violence at the festival, and the implications for future musical gatherings.

331. Walters, Barry. "Nü Metal and Woodstock '99." *The Rock History Reader.* Ed. Theo Cateforis. New York: Routledge, 2007. 313–315.

Draws from the author's *Washington Post* article analyzing the events at Woodstock '99 (Barry Walters, "The Arson is Blowin' in the Wind: Why *Woodstock '99* Devolved into a Frat-Style Free-For-All," The *Washington Post*, August 8, 1999, p. G1). Notes the mythology of the original Woodstock Music and Art Fair was shattered by the Woodstock '99 audiences' desire for "angry, aggressive music." Suggests the music by such acts as Limp Bizkit, Korn, and the Red Hot Chili Peppers both fueled and reflected the psychology behind the riots, looting, sexual assaults, and mayhem.

Articles

332. Abril, Carlos R. "Functions of a National Anthem in Society and Education: A Sociocultural Perspective." *Bulletin of the Council for Research in Music Education* 172 (2007): 69–87.

Examines *The Star Spangled Banner* in its role as a national anthem. Provides the historical background and uses "various sociocultural conceptualizations of music and social functions as guideposts around which to wrap historical and autobiographical narratives" in order to reject "absolutist portrayals" in school music curriculum. Points to Jimi Hendrix's performance of the piece at the Woodstock Music and Art Fair as being a representation of the freedom to "ascribe personal meaning to the song in transmission and appropriation." Notes at the time the performance was considered by many as too severe a transgression to be accepted. Observes now the same performance is considered ground breaking and profound.

333. Araújo, Samuel M. "Brega: Music and Conflict in Urban Brazil." *Latin American Music Review* 9.1 (1988): 50–89. https://doi.org/10.2307/779999

Uses the "crowd rain chant" from the motion picture *Woodstock* as a brief point of reference in exploring the evolution of brega, a form of Brazilian popular music grounded in socio-economic roots. Insists "brega opens a quite provoking field to those interested in the ways music expresses the social dynamics within the global village."

334. Auslander, Philip. "Good Old Rock and Roll: Performing the 1950s in the 1970s." *Journal of Popular Music Studies* 15.2 (2003): 166–194. https://doi.org/10.1111/j.1533–1598.2003.00003.x   http://homes.lmc.gatech.edu/~auslander/publications/good old rock and roll.pdf

Explores two poles of the ideological continuum between authenticity and inauthenticity in rock music culture. Uses the music group Sha Na Na and the musician John Lennon to represent the two extremes. Observes John Lennon's performances of rock and roll music from the 1950s are authentic because he had a personal biographical connection to the music. Claims Sha Na Na's performance at the Woodstock Music and Art Fair served to anticipate a "historical discontinuity between countercultural rock and what came after it." States the performance was a harbinger of change in popular music culture, anticipating glam and punk rock. Discusses the "historical irony" of Sha Na Na's appearance at Woodstock. Sums the significance by observing, unlike all the other acts at the festival, Sha Na Na presented a theatrical and constructed personae without an "authentic personal and historical connection to rock and roll." Part II of the article continues by discussing instances in which musicians of the 1960s with authentic connections to the music of the 1950s created alter egos in order to perform rock and roll music (e.g., Frank Zappa; Beach Boys). Notes this places them between the two poles. Connects the ideological continuum to that of modernism versus postmodernism.

335. Chang, Vanessa. "Records that Play: The Present Past in Sampling Practice." *Popular Music* 28.2 (2009): 143–159. https://doi.org/10.1017/s0261143009001755

>   Examines the theoretical basis of discourse surrounding the practice of sampling and posits the sampled is a space where "the past both defines the present and is effaced by it." Refers to previous scholarship regarding Jimi Hendrix's performance of *The Star Spangled Banner* at the Woodstock Music and Art Fair. Reports that by referencing the composition *Taps* through integration into his rendition of the national anthem, Hendrix created a sign "encoded with a kind of external logic, its meaning determined by its context." Claims Hendrix was able to subvert the semiotic system of the national anthem and "the referent of the cited song, the nation, is present, even as its internal nationalistic structure is made absent." Asserts sampling makes disparate source material coherent and serves as a cultural metaphor with "musical space doubling for social space." Concludes "sampling creates a tradition that involves the past without deferring to its structures and limitations, restoring a revised mode of agency to the practice," thus evoking nostalgia without recreating the event.

336. Clague, Mark. "'This is America': Jimi Hendrix's Star Spangled Banner Journey as Psychedelic Citizenship." *Journal of the Society for American Music* 8.4 (2014): 435–478. https://doi.org/10.1017/s1752196314000364

>   Characterizes Jimi Hendrix's performance of *The Star Spangled Banner* at the Woodstock Music and Art Fair as being "an expression of transcendent political resistance" representing "the most powerful symbol of rock's potential for protest." Analyzes in detail Hendrix's "artistic engagement" with the national anthem by tracing his history of playing, recording, writing about, and discussing it. Looks comprehensively at two years of performances, including stage banter, to gain understanding of Hendrix's political perspective and rhetoric. Delves into Hendrix's personal military history (he enlisted in 1961). Reveals it was not planned Hendrix would play the national anthem at Woodstock, yet it has become one the most famous performances in the history of rock music. Suggests he added it to the set as a "celebration of possibility" inspired by his positive experience at the festival. Describes Hendrix's rendition of the *The Star Spangled Banner* at Woodstock in great detail, breaking the performance down almost note by note. Contrasts this event with previous live renderings of the piece, building the case that on this particular day the musician was making a statement of

affirmation rather than protest. Recounts Hendrix's interview about the performance shortly afterwards on *The Dick Cavett Show*. Comments on how he enhanced the tune with "increasing amounts of ornamentation" for post-Woodstock renderings. Concludes by noting how the Woodstock version, having been highlighted as the capstone performance in the motion picture *Woodstock*, has become engrained in American culture as a melding of both the artistic and social imagination.

337. Gracyk, Theodore. "Meanings of Songs and Meanings of Song Performances." *Journal of Aesthetics & Art Criticism* 71.1 (2013): 23–33.

Purports to demonstrate "the interplay of semantics and pragmatics" in generating differing meanings by different performances. Offers meanings of songs are fixed, but each performance of a song can have different meanings. Contends musical performances are rich in meaning due to the semantic information associated with musical structure, thus creating numerous possibilities for pragmatic contextual interpretation. Highlights the Jimi Hendrix performance of *The Star Spangled Banner* at the Woodstock Music and Art Fair as one example of how a performance can offer new connotations without altering the intended meaning of the music being performed. Hendrix made a political statement with his rendering of the composition, thus exploiting a cultural context to "generate pragmatic implications that are not part of the musical work."

338. Henderson, David. "Jimi Hendrix Deep within the Blues and Alive Onstage at Woodstock — 25 Years After Death." *African American Review* 29 (1995): 213–216. https://doi.org/10.2307/3042293

Reviews Jimi Hendrix musicianship as a blues guitarist and comments on his performance at the Woodstock Music and Art Fair. Notes near the end of his performance, Hendrix was "delving deeply into the improvisational mode where blues and jazz truly intersect." Comments on the band accompanying Hendrix during his Woodstock gig. Contends his talent for playing the blues placed him "well within the pantheon of blues greats," including Albert King, Muddy Waters and Elmore James. Reproduces some poetic text written by Hendrix at the Woodstock festival.

339. Kaufmann, Donald. "Woodstock: The Color of Sound." *Journal of Ethnic Studies* 2.3 (1974): 32–49.

Argues the Woodstock Music and Art Fair resolved the question of African-American music acceptance into mainstream popular culture. Claims the festival demonstrated African-American music "had finally learned to coexist with white electronics" resulting in a "mulatto sound." Delves into an extensive history of black music in America. Articulates the ways in which white America has periodically discovered black music and integrated the sounds into its own popular music. Predicts once the Woodstock generation comes of age and assumes political power, cultural assumptions about distinctions between black music and white music will be gone.

340. Konečni, Vladimir J., Rebekah A. Wanic, and Amber Brown. "Emotional and Aesthetic Antecedents and Consequences of Music-Induced Thrills." *American Journal of Psychology* 120.4 (2007): 619–643. https://doi.org/10.2307/20445428 http://konecni.ucsd.edu/pdf/2007 K., W., and B., Thrills-Chills AJP.pdf

> Utilizes a recording of Jimi Hendrix (1942–1970) performing *The Star Spangled Banner* at the Woodstock Music and Art Fair to conduct controlled experiments exploring "the significance of music-induced thrills." Uses various aesthetics (e.g., national anthems, objects, paintings) to increase the thrill response to the music of Sergei Rachmaninoff (1873–1943) and Joseph Haydn (1732–1809). Concludes "thrills may often accompany profound aesthetic experiences and provide their physiological underpinning, yet themselves be of limited psychological significance."

341. Manderson, Desmond. "Towards Law and Music." *Law and Critique* 25.3 (2014): 311–317. https://doi.org/10.1007/s10978-014-9142-8

> Assesses "scholarly directions in the interdisciplinary field of law and music." Illustrates the "vocabulary" of music through the example of Jimi Hendrix's rendition of *The Star Spangled Banner* at the Woodstock Music and Art Fair. Contends Hendrix performed a juxtaposition between America's polar demographics (the old and the new) and political ideologies at that time in history. Notes through his music Hendrix was able to contrast "patriotism with violence, and victimhood with aggression." Suggests he was articulating legal subjectivity through his music.

342. Marom, Maya K. "Spiritual Moments in Music Therapy: A Qualitative Study of the Music Therapist's Experience." *Qualitative Inquiries in Music Therapy* 1 (2004): 37–76. http://www.barcelonapublishers. com/resources/QIMTV1/QIMT2004Volume1_Marom.pdf

> Investigates "spiritual moments in different music therapy settings" in order to examine the "personal experience of the music therapists involved in them." Utilizes a qualitative research methodology. Explains

therapists were asked to describe sessions in which the "therapeutic process became spiritual in nature." Examines, among other things, the role of music in these experiences. Offers one example in which a client was frightened to hear the entire recording of Jimi Hendrix's performance of *The Star Spangled Banner* at the Woodstock Music and Art Fair. Notes following a session in which therapist and client listened to the entire piece, therapist was surprised to "witness a client have a life-changing spiritual experience to the sounds of this music." Concludes any type of music can create a transformative experience, as long as it has relevance to the individual.

343. Maxile, Horace J., Jr. "Signs, Symphonies, Signifyin(g): African-American Cultural Topics as Analytical Approach to the Music of Black Composers." *Black Music Research Journal* 28.1 (2008): 124–138.

Calls for more scholarship on black composers in terms of "criticism, interpretation, and analysis of concert works." Focuses on reviewing and expanding upon current theories in order to address the "analysis/ interpretation gap" regarding concert performances by African Americans. Points to Jimi Hendrix's performance of *The Star Spangled Banner* at the Woodstock Music and Art Fair as an example of "signifying" (e.g., satire, reverence, politics). Contends Hendrix transformed the national anthem with bent tones, wide vibrato, etc., thus utilizing "African-American cultural emblems." As a result, Hendrix addressed the social and political climate of the late 1960s.

344. Silverman, Alan. "Music at Woodstock." *AES: Journal of the Audio Engineering Society* 55.4 (2007): 308–309.

Reports on a meeting of the New York Section of the Audio Engineering Society (AES) held at the Digital Cinema Dubbing Stage (December 12, 2006). Highlights a behind-the-scenes technical history of the Woodstock Music and Art Fair. Festival technical director Chris Langhart, sound contractor Bill Hanley, promoter Michael Lang, and on-site staff John Chester provide first-person descriptions and explanations. Comments on segments from the motion picture *Woodstock* used to illustrate the sound recording techniques utilized at the concert.

345. Turino, Thomas. "Signs of Imagination, Identity, and Experience: A Peircian Semiotic Theory for Music." *Ethnomusicology* 43.2 (1999): 221–255. https://doi.org/10.2307/852734

Offers Charles Sanders Peirce's semiotic theory "as an avenue for understanding musical affectivity, different parts of ourselves and

experiences, and the special potentials of music for the construction
of personal and social identities." In particular, suggests the theory
is "revolutionary for understanding the social effects of music, art,
expressive culture, and people's myriad ways of experiencing the
world." As one musical example of creative indexing, the author points
to Jimi Hendrix's rendering of *The Star Spangled Banner* at the Woodstock
Music and Art Fair. Notes the use of guitar feedback and distortion
(counterculture ethos) during the performance is juxtaposed with the
composition's "nationalistic contexts" (patriotic ethos), thus "shifts
of accent, rhythm, and phrasing, and the use of rock-rift conventions"
express sarcasm.

346. Waksman, Steve. "Black Sound, Black Body: Jimi Hendrix, the
Electric Guitar, and the Meanings of Blackness." *Popular Music and
Society* 23.1 (1999): 75–113. https://doi.org/10.1080/03007769908591726

Considers in this lengthy article Jimi Hendrix's relationship to "blackness"
as a category of representation, in terms of his music, performance style,
and technology. Contrasts Hendrix's interpretation of *The Star Spangled
Banner* at the Woodstock Music and Art Fair with a performance of the
same tune earlier in the same year. Claims the Woodstock rendition
of the national anthem was "a full-fledged reinvention of it, such that
the original can never be heard quite the same way again." Suggests in
breaking from a traditional performance of this particular song, Hendrix
interjected a stylistic evocation of African music. Considers also the
intersections of race and gender in Hendrix's style of performance.

Videos

347. *Jimi Hendrix: Live at Woodstock.* Prod. Janie Hendrix and John
McDermott. Experience Hendrix L.L.C., 2010.

Updated Blu-ray edition of a video first released in the 1990s. Features
all of the existing film footage of Jimi Hendrix at the Woodstock Music
and Art Fair, re-edited and presented in the original performance
sequence. Includes a second disc of interviews with the musicians and
others, alternate camera angles of the performance, and a post-concert
interview with Jimi Hendrix (September 3, 1969) discussing *The Star
Spangled Banner.*

348. *Woodstock: The Lost Performances.* Warner Home Video, 1991.

Contains over an hour's worth of Woodstock Music and Art Fair
performances not seen in the original 1970 motion picture, *Woodstock.*

Some of the acts included here were not featured in the original film. Highlights are songs by Janis Joplin, Melanie, Tim Hardin, The Band, Richie Havens, Joe Cocker, Arlo Guthrie, Canned Heat and others. Compiled for the 20th anniversary of the festival.

Recordings

349. *Woodstock: Music from the Original Soundtrack and More.* Cotillion, 1970.

Contains the first release of selected live recordings of music, stage announcements, and crowd noise from the Woodstock Music and Art Fair. Followed by the album *Woodstock Two*, released in 1971. In 1994 additional musical performances were added for a 4 CD box set release, *Woodstock: Three Days of Peace and Music*. In 2009, more content was added and released as a 6 CD box set, *Woodstock—40 Years On: Back to Yasgur's Farm.*

350. *Woodstock: Three Days of Peace and Music.* Atlantic, 1994.

Presents the third release of selected live recordings of music from the 1969 Woodstock Music and Art Fair. Follows the albums *Woodstock: Music from the Original Soundtrack and More* (1970) and *Woodstock Two* (1971). Contains additional musical performances packaged in a 4 CD box set release. Followed by a 6 CD box set, *Woodstock—40 Years On: Back to Yasgur's Farm* (2009). Program notes by David Fricke.

351. *Woodstock—40 Years On: Back to Yasgur's Farm.* Rhino, 2009.

Presents the fourth release of live recordings of music from the 1969 Woodstock music festival. Follows the albums *Woodstock: Music from the Original Soundtrack and More* (1970), *Woodstock Two* (1971), and *Woodstock: Three Days of Peace and Music* (1994). Contains additional musical performances, all packaged in a 6 CD box set release.

352. *Woodstock Two.* Atlantic, 1971.

Presents the second release of selected live recordings of music from the 1969 Woodstock Music and Art Fair. Follows the album *Woodstock: Music from the Original Soundtrack and More* (1970). Followed by a 4 CD box set release, *Woodstock: Three Days of Peace and Music* (1994) and then by a 6 CD box set, *Woodstock—40 Years On: Back to Yasgur's Farm* (2009).

Film

Books

353. Biskind, Peter. *Easy Riders, Raging Bulls: How the Sex-Drugs-and-Rock 'n' Roll Generation Saved Hollywood*. New York: Simon & Schuster, 1998.

Offers a history on the coming of age of the counterculture's most prominent filmmakers. Covers all the major players and their contributions. Includes Fred Weintraub recalling briefly how he managed to get the motion picture *Woodstock* produced in an era when most, if not all, rock concert films had been less than successful. Notes as a result Weintraub became "the executive in charge of alternative lifestyles" at Warner Bros.

354. Brode, Douglas. *From Walt to Woodstock: How Disney Created the Counterculture*. Austin, TX: University of Texas Press, 2004.

Uses the Woodstock Music and Art Fair as an allegorical reference to the 1960s counterculture representing an end product of American youth raised on Disney films. Admits this runs counter to the conventional wisdom of Disney projects avoiding controversy in exchange for commercial gain. Posits Disney films taught the youth of America to worship Plato's "Good" and this was manifested in the behaviors of Woodstock attendees. Provides a textual analysis of specific Disney films, suggests an oeuvre expressing "the single imagination of the auteur," and conducts a socio-political evaluation of the oeuvre within a historical context. Shows how Disney films introduced themes which later came to define the counterculture, such as pacifism and "return to nature" virtues.

     http://dx.doi.org/10.11647/OBP.0105.05

355. Cagin, Seth, and Philip Dray. *Hollywood Films of the Seventies: Sex, Drugs, Violence, Rock 'n' Roll & Politics*. New York: Harper & Row, 1984.

Discusses, in part, the motion picture *Woodstock* as being "profoundly ambivalent, containing hints of dark pessimism buried within its professed ethos of affirmation." Questions whether the film, along with other similar "youth-cult" cinema such as *Gimme Shelter, Easy Rider* and *Zabriskie Point*, turned sentimental nostalgia into a marketing concept. Explores the behind-the-scenes murky acquisition of film rights for *Woodstock* and the machinations of obtaining a suitable Motion Picture Association of America (MPAA) rating for the movie. Covers other controversies associated with *Woodstock*, mainly focusing on issues of commercial exploitation. Continues by noting all of this became "overshadowed by the blast of moral indignation" with the release of the motion picture *Gimme Shelter* by the Maysles brothers.

356. Denisoff, R. Serge, and William D. Romanowski. *Risky Business: Rock in Film*. New Brunswick, NJ: Transaction, 1991.

Discusses "rockumentaries" (rock music film documentaries), from *The T.A.M.I. Show* through *Imagine: John Lennon*. Offers insight into the particular business deal that resulted ultimately in the motion picture *Woodstock*. Comments on the critical and financial success of the film. Provides a history of the movie's commercial life. Contrasts the film with the motion picture *Gimme Shelter*. Includes commentary on other motion pictures such as *Monterey Pop, Let It Be, The Concert for Bangla Desh, Stop Making Sense,* and *Rattle and Hum*.

357. Friedman, Lawrence S. *The Cinema of Martin Scorsese*. New York: Continuum, 1997.

Chronicles the career of Martin Scorsese. Refers to the motion picture *Woodstock* as "arguably the greatest concert film ever made." States the movie's director, Michael Wadleigh, hired Scorsese as an assistant director and supervising editor. Claims the technical accomplishments of the film have been mostly ignored. Suggests the real success of the movie is due to Scorsese's editing. Lists the "brilliantly edited sequences" as being those performances by Joan Baez, Joe Cocker, Sly and the Family Stone, and Crosby, Stills, Nash & Young. Demonstrates the high quality editing skills of Scorsese and Thelma Schoonmaker by citing as contrast the mostly unedited Jimi Hendrix sequence added to the "director's cut" version of the film.

358. Grant, Barry Keith. *The Hollywood Film Musical*. Malden, MA: Wiley-Blackwell, 2012.

Presents first a "concise history of the genre and an overview of the critical debates about" film musicals. Offers both historical and critical overviews, followed by chapters devoted to the analysis of specific movies. Includes an in depth examination of the motion picture *Woodstock*. Notes the film was edited using 1,210 hours of footage. States documentaries are constructed representations and, therefore, claims *Woodstock* is not simply a random assemblage of scenes but rather a depiction of "the musical expression of the counter-culture's rejection of middle-class values and lifestyle in favor of a more open and accepting society." Observes how the film "builds a sense of community through a resistance to the Vietnam War," celebrates sexual liberation, and creates unity in the face of, literally, a gathering storm. Comments on how, at the same time, the filmmakers seem aware the festival's "utopian community was an ephemeral achievement" and not possible to perpetuate.

359. Kato, M. T. *From Kung Fu to Hip Hop: Globalization, Revolution, and Popular Culture*. Albany, NY: State University of New York Press, 2007.

Observes the motion picture *Woodstock* not only captured the performances of musicians, but also "captured the cultural milieu" of the youth movement unfolding with the event. Asserts the film also attempted to contain symbolically the counterculture movement, best represented in the portrayal of Jimi Hendrix's performance. Claims Hendrix's use of a new band at the festival, musicians specifically selected for freestyle jamming, was a "sincere tribute to the original motive and intent of the Woodstock Music and Art Fair." Believes Hendrix's performance of *The Star Spangled Banner* "offered a concrete reference point to which the totality of Woodstock was dedicated and upon which the counterculture as a whole was founded." States the way in which Hendrix's set was filmed and edited for the motion picture, essentially excluding the other members of the band and the audience, was "meant to be a eulogy for the rebellious souls of the counterculture." Suggests the "politics of cinematography" deployed in the film was a corporate strategy intent on containing the counterculture in a specific time and place.

360. Kellner, Douglas. *Media Culture: Cultural Studies, Identity, and Politics between the Modern and the Postmodern*. London: Routledge, 1995. https://doi.org/10.4324/9780203205808

Proclaims "a media culture has emerged in which images, sounds, and spectacles" shape political views and social behaviors, thus helping create identity. Explores the consequences of media colonization. Contends the motion pictures *Easy Rider* and *Woodstock* "transcoded the sixties discourses." Claims the latter film provided "figural action" showing musicians as cultural heroes, promoters as benevolent benefactors, and audience as counterculture participants. Suggests these two motion pictures reduced 1960s political activism to cultural style which in turn made it easy to co-opt and exploit the counterculture, eventually leading to its demise.

361. King, Claire Sisco. *Washed in Blood: Male Sacrifice, Trauma, and the Cinema*. New Brunswick, NJ: Rutgers University Press, 2012.

Studies the "logic of traumatic heroism" within the cultural context of motion pictures. Discusses the film *Omega Man* and its use of a character watching the movie *Woodstock* as "offering ethical imperatives and political critiques specific to its historical context." Suggests the character's viewing of *Woodstock* represents "the countercultural rejection of the hegemonic masculine attitudes that celebrate violence and war-making" in favor of gentleness.

362. Leff, Leonard J., and Jerold L. Simmons. *The Dame in the Kimono: Hollywood, Censorship and the Production Code*. Lexington, KY: University Press of Kentucky, 2001.

Presents the history of motion picture ratings and censorship. Mentions succinctly a debate over which rating to assign to the film *Woodstock*, "R" versus "PG." Implies the deciding factor was the repeated use of the word "fuck" during "The Fish Cheer" by Country Joe McDonald.

363. Marcus, Greil. *In the Fascist Bathroom: Punk in Pop Music 1977–1992*. Cambridge, MA: Harvard University Press, 1993.

Notes in brief the "imaginative camera work and editing" on "nine otherwise-unlistenable minutes" of the performance by Ten Years After in the motion picture *Woodstock*. Compares this to the motion picture *No Nukes* in which there is a noticeable lack of creative filmmaking.

364. McElhaney, Joe. *Albert Maysles*. Ed. James Naremore. Contemporary Film Directors. Urbana, IL: University of Illinois Press, 2009.

Examines the documentary film work of Albert Maysles. Compares and contrasts the motion picture *Woodstock* with Maysles's film *Gimme Shelter* documenting the disastrous Altamont Speedway concert. Describes *Woodstock* as reinforcing the concept of the festival as having been "part of the natural world that surrounds it rather than an intrusion." The politeness of Woodstock participants is emphasized, thus insinuating the counterculture coexists with mainstream culture, rather than in opposition to it. Claims *Gimme Shelter* presents the youth culture lacking utopian wonder. Observes nudity and sexuality, as representations of nature or being natural, are portrayed in *Gimme Shelter* as uncontrolled animal disorder. Suggests the Maysles film presents audience members dancing using variable camera speeds in order to "giving the dances a strange, unnatural rhythm and movement." Includes a filmography.

365. Monaco, James. *American Film Now: The People, the Power, the Money, the Movies.* New York: Oxford University Press, 1979.

Provides wide-ranging insight into multiple aspects of the movie-making industry. Credits Martin Scorsese as the real creative force behind the motion picture *Woodstock*. Claims it was one thing to shoot an overwhelming amount of footage, but it took talent to give it shape and pace within an acceptable running time. Asserts the film is "one of the most notable models of the craft of editing since the Steenbeck editing table was invented."

366. Raymond, Marc. *Hollywood's New Yorker: The Making of Martin Scorsese.* Albany, NY: State University of New York Press, 2013.

Analyzes Martin Scorsese's role in the culture of motion pictures. Inspects concisely Martin Scorsese's degree of involvement with the making of the film *Woodstock*. Reports Scorsese was an assistant director for the shoot and then worked on editing the movie. Notes some think he was apathetic to the counterculture ethos, thus allowing him a certain amount of "personal indifference." Counters others consider his work on the film to be political. Suggests attributing too much of the film's success to Scorsese is "flawed and yet unfortunately common auteurist logic" in which the criterion for a film being labeled authentic art is how the maker "must be deemed worthy" (as Scorsese's post-*Woodstock* career attests). Asserts "the question of who the authentic artist actually is assumes greater importance, even within obviously collective activity, for if one is not an artist, one is simply personnel."

367. *Woodstock: An Inside Look at the Movie that Shook Up the World and Defined a Generation.* Ed. Dale Bell. Studio City, CA: Michael Wise, 1999.

Provides detailed insight into the making of the motion picture *Woodstock* using a large collection of brief interviews and essays by those involved and by some of the artists captured in the film. Contains sixty-nine chapters by thirty-nine contributors compiled into a "*cinéma verité* book." Discusses every aspect of the festival, post-production on the movie, and the social and artistic impact. Describes how the film crew was pulled together. Explains the innovations required in order to fulfill the vision of the filmmakers. Offers perceptions on the sometimes difficult working relationship with Warner Bros. Studio during post-production. Communicates the political environment during the screening at the 1970 Cannes Film Festival in light of the Kent State shootings. Includes a foreword by Martin Scorsese, a "where are they now" section, and numerous black and white photographs.

Chapters

368. Arnold, Gina. "Nobody's Army: Contradictory Cultural Rhetoric in Woodstock and Gimme Shelter." *Countercultures and Popular Music.* Eds. Sheila Whiteley and Jedediah Sklower. Farnham, U.K.: Ashgate, 2014. 123–137. https://doi.org/10.4324/9781315574479 https://ia800205. us.archive.org/17/items/Countercultures_and_Popular_Music_by_ Jedediah_Sklower_Sheila_Whiteley/Countercultures_and_Popular_ Music_by_Jedediah_Sklower_Sheila_Whiteley.pdf

> Investigates "the genesis of the powerlessness and lack of direction that rock crowds represent." Looks at the motion pictures *Woodstock* and *Gimme Shelter* as sources of rhetoric which create a misperception of concert audiences being rebellious when, in fact, they are "largely docile, passive and conservative." Offers these two films, one documenting 1969's Woodstock Music and Art Fair (*Woodstock*) and the other the Altamont Speedway concert (*Gimme Shelter*), serve to reinforce notions of democracy and capitalism. Argues *Woodstock* does not document an event, such as newsreel might, but instead creates a narrative and an ideology. Explores the notion of duality represented by means of the film, citing examples of such concepts as conventional versus unconventional and technology versus nature. Claims the *Gimme Shelter* uses similar rhetoric strategies as *Woodstock*. Concludes both films portray the relationship between promoters/musicians/vendors and consumers in such a way as to create the moral acceptance of the market economy within the youth culture. Notes the films also establish as a commodity the intangibleness of an experience.

369. Baker, Michael Brendan. "Martin Scorsese and the Music Documentary." *A Companion to Martin Scorsese.* Ed. Aaron Baker. Chichester, U.K.: Wiley Blackwell, 2015. 239–258. https://doi.org/10. 1002/9781118585344.ch11

Explores Martin Scorsese's relationship to rock music as expressed in his documentaries. Examines the evolution of rockumentaries, starting with the *T.A.M.I. Show* (1965). Claims the motion picture *Woodstock* "enshrined the North American counterculture of the 1960s." Notes a major significance of *Woodstock* is the way in which it highlights the audience as an essential element of the documented experience. Offers Scorsese's contributions and efforts in making *Woodstock* established his "imprint on the rockumentary genre." Focuses on Scorsese's role as assistant director, his work on capturing the stage performances, and the use of split-screen to portray audience reactions. Continues with discussions of other Scorsese motion picture documentaries, including *The Last Waltz* (featuring The Band), *No Direction Home: Bob Dylan*, and *Shine a Light* (featuring The Rolling Stones). States Scorsese was central to the formation of the rockumentary genre, especially its form and structure.

370. Barsam, Richard M. "The New Nonfiction Film: 1960–1970." *Nonfiction Film: A Critical History.* New York: E. P. Dutton, 1973. 247–295.

Writes on the resurgence of nonfiction film production during the 1960s. Asserts the motion pictures *Woodstock* and *Gimme Shelter* are juxtaposed in the culture of rock music festivals, in their symbolism of the 1960s counterculture, and in approaches to filmmaking. States the former represents "love, music, and fun" while the latter conveys "hate, music, and horror." Claims *Woodstock* is a subjective documentary and *Gimme Shelter* "comes as close to pure nonfiction film as any film has." Notes *Woodstock* has uneven quality of footage, varying greatly from performer to performer. Observes *Woodstock* is more commercially oriented in its presentation than *Gimme Shelter*. Concludes the success of these two motion pictures created increased support for nonfiction film projects.

371. Bennett, Andy. "Everybody's Happy, Everybody's Free: Representation and Nostalgia in the Woodstock Film." *Remembering Woodstock.* Ed. Andy Bennett. Aldershot, U.K.: Ashgate, 2004. 43–54.

Evaluates the significance of the motion picture *Woodstock* as not only a documentation of the festival, but also as a production of nostalgia. Begins with a brief description of the loose and challenging way in which the event was captured on film. Discusses how editing, sequencing scenes, and the use of split-screen removes selected actual events from their original context and makes them iconic in shaping perceptions and recollections of the festival. Explores how rock music by the late 1960s had come to represent the counterculture ethos of community between musician and audience, but in reality was a business firmly grounded in capitalism. Traces the evolution into mythology of an idealized vision of the counterculture as presented in the film *Woodstock* which now serves as a nostalgia trigger for an idealized time that never existed in reality. Offers that the "film continuously plays down the mundane in favour of the spectacular" resulting in the representation of the festival as a pinnacle statement on 1960s' counterculture.

372. Ebert, Roger. "Woodstock." *Awake in the Dark: The Best of Roger Ebert.* Chicago: University of Chicago Press, 2006. 267–271. https://doi.org/10.7208/chicago/9780226182063.001.0001

> Reviews (from May 3, 1970) the motion picture *Woodstock*. Asserts the film "may be the best documentary ever made in America." States this documentary is more than a movie on rock music; it is an "archeological study" on a briefly formed civilization. Claims the film is remarkable because in conveys realistically the experience of having been at the Woodstock Music and Art Fair. Comments on the editorial skill of providing an objective, if not neutral, perspective on the event. Notes *Woodstock* captures the musician/audience inter-participation of the performances. Reveals being moved by Joan Baez's set. Marvels at the film capturing and presenting a folk singer's act (Richie Havens) just as powerfully as any of those by the rock groups. Suggests the use of split screen is more successful in this film than others because it is used to advance the narrative.

373. Edgar, Robert, Kirsty Fairclough-Isaacs, and Benjamin Halligan. "Music Seen: The Formats and Functions of the Music Documentary." *The Music Documentary: Acid Rock to Electropop.* Eds. Robert Edgar, Kirsty Fairclough-Isaacs, and Benjamin Halligan. New York: Routledge, 2013. 1–21. https://doi.org/10.4324/9780203118689

> Focuses on the transformative arrival of music videos intended for television audiences. Notes that the *Woodstock* film and others of the same period were essentially documenting musical events with "the cameras engaged in reportage, the musicians primarily engaged in the live delivery of their music." The premise of these films being one of "an active and nuanced dialogue between performances and audiences." Claims that in the video age image comes before the music. Continues the discussion by noting a hybrid evolution throughout the 1980s to a preference for more stylized live performances and then on to the cult of celebrity. States contemporary music documentaries help create a "celebrity/star brand" by offering a presentation of "manufactured

authenticity." Concludes by noting the music documentary "persists as both an index of, and access to, the certainties and the vagaries of popular culture."

374. MacDonald, Stephen. "Woodstock: One for the Money." *The Documentary Tradition: From Nanook to Woodstock.* Ed. Lewis Jacobs. New York: Hopkinson and Blake, 1971. 492–493.

Reprints an article from *The Wall Street Journal* (March 27, 1970) commenting on the motion picture *Woodstock*. Notes the apparent purpose of the film is to celebrate, rather than examine, the Woodstock Music and Art Fair. Observes the vignettes of the attendees (e.g., dancing and skinny-dipping) make the event seem very appealing, but the interviews are disturbing. Claims attendees come across as "wholly inarticulate." Notes the local citizens are portrayed as being "quaint old squares." Concludes by noting how the film highlights the one thing proven by the festival, which is the "commercially exploitable" nature of the counterculture.

375. Niemi, Robert. "Music History on Film and Television: Woodstock (1970)." *History in the Media: Film and Television.* Santa Barbara, CA: ABC-CLIO, 2006. 258–260.

Expresses some distain for the motion picture *Woodstock*, describing it as "a sprawling, overlong mess, exciting and boring by turns." Comments that the film was not intended to simply document the event, but to "celebrate the hippie/counterculture in all its supposed peace-loving, sensuous, gaudy vibrancy." Suggests by the time the film was released in 1970 the "hippie ethos had already died" citing as evidence the Manson murders and the violent Altamont Speedway concert. Includes a reproduction of a poster promoting the event, not the film.

376. Romberg, Chris, and Keith Roberts Sargent. "Interview with Jimi Hendrix." *Hendrix on Hendrix: Interviews and Encounters with Jimi Hendrix.* Ed. Steven Roby. Chicago: Chicago Review Press, 2012. 309–316.

Transcribes an interview from the Armed Forces Radio Network (September 1970) in which Hendrix is asked to comment on his appearance in the motion picture *Woodstock* and especially on his performance of *The Star Spangled Banner* in the film. Hendrix's responses are mostly evasive.

377. Saffle, Michael. "Retrospective Compilations: (Re)Defining the Music Documentary." *The Music Documentary: Acid Rock to Electropop.* Eds.

Robert Edgar, Kirsty Fairclough-Isaacs, and Benjamin Halligan. New York: Routledge, 2013. 42–54. https://doi.org/10.4324/9780203118689

> Evaluates music documentaries "in terms of accessibility, authenticity, film history, media issues, musical styles, and political-social-cultural goals ranging from avant-garde experimentation to postmodern infotainment." Points to the motion picture *Woodstock* as an example of how music documentaries tend to be about contemporary events and not as retrospective as other documentaries. At the time of its original release, *Woodstock* reported on a still current newsworthy event. Commenting on the 1994 and 2009 re-releases of *Woodstock*, with much more footage added each time, the author offers the film as an example of a remade documentary. Notes *Woodstock* contains footage of the photographers and interviewers, thus making the film a "simultaneously informative and entertaining, authentic and self-consciously arch."

378. Saunders, Dave. "In Search of Elysium." *Direct Cinema: Observational Documentary and the Politics of the Sixties.* London: Wallflower Press, 2007. 99–125.

> Examines American *cinema verite* of the 1960s for its richness in "subjective creativity and discursive potency." Provides the context of the Vietnam War and associated domestic political unrest in order to introduce a discussion on the motion picture *Woodstock*. Mentions filmmaker Michael Wadleigh's financial incentives for his crew if the film were to be successful. Analyzes in detail the movie, scene by scene, from the pastoral views of readying the site and the audience's arrival through the selected performances portrayed on the screen to the final set by Jimi Hendrix, suggesting his articulation of *The Star Spangled Banner* represented the counterculture deconstructing itself. Concludes the film's theme is "all this fleeting happiness is bought at a price to our conscience and morals."

379. Wright, Julie Lobalzo. "The Good, the Bad, and the Ugly '60s: The Opposing Gazes of Woodstock and Gimme Shelter." *The Music Documentary: Acid Rock to Electropop.* Eds. Robert Edgar, Kirsty Fairclough-Isaacs, and Benjamin Halligan. New York: Routledge, 2013. 71–86. https://doi.org/10.4324/9780203118689

> Compares and contrasts two documentary motion pictures, *Woodstock* (Woodstock Music and Art Fair) and *Gimme Shelter* (Altamont Speedway concert). Offers the former as the "zenith of the counterculture movement" and the latter as "its violent end." Contends these two films "helped

shape both the 'Direct Cinema' movement and the 'rockumentary' genre." Draws the distinction of "communal gaze" (*Woodstock*) and "disconnecting gaze" (*Gimme Shelter*). Examines the two films from three perspectives: setting, crowd, and performances. *Woodstock* creates a setting with scenes of open, green fields thus establishing the "environment as idyllic, peaceful, and agrarian." The crowd shots are expansive and portray a sense of community. The performances shown on screen emphasize collaboration with the audience using wide frame shots of people clapping to the music and dancing. *Gimme Shelter* makes heavy use of tightly framed shots for the setting, the crowd, and the performances, thus evoking claustrophobia and individualism. Claims memories of the events captured in the two films have been "shaped by the nature of these aesthetic strategies." States it is important to acknowledge the film texts are presented with intention.

Articles

380. Barron, Arthur. "Ken Edwards Memorial Address." *Journal of the University Film Association* 21.3 (1969): 77–80.

Poses the question of relevance for filmmakers in light of the Woodstock Music and Art Fair and "the profound revolution in life style and values." Bases question on the author's then recent experience at the festival. Speaks from the perspective of the film division of Columbia University. Categorizes motion pictures into three traditions: reporting, instructing, and "human revelation." Calls for filmmakers to focus on human revelation in which the film experience is the focal point, rather than the informational content it may be conveying. Defines human revelation films as experimental, not didactic, and sharing the human experience on an emotional level. Reasons this will serve the purpose that all art serves which is to make the joy and grief of one comprehensible to all.

381. Bodroghkozy, Aniko. "Reel Revolutionaries: An Examination of Hollywood's Cycle of 1960s Youth Rebellion Films." *Cinema Journal* 41.3 (2002): 38–58. https://doi.org/10.1353/cj.2002.0007 http://www.asu.edu/courses/fms394/readings-biddinger/L6 bodroghkozy.rebellionfilms.pdf

Dissects attempts by Hollywood studios to lure youth audiences during the late 1960s and early 1970s by using films about political activism and youth protest. Includes unfavorable responses to these actions as reflected in underground newspapers. Observes Hollywood's "schizophrenic" attempts to negotiate ideologies when marketing to the youth culture. Notes the reaction to the film *Woodstock* was less critical since it was regarded as a documentary and, therefore, considered less contrived. However, criticism erupted over the marketing of the film because of the "blatant example of cooptation" for purposes of commercialization. Describes how successful pickets and boycotts were organized and the related consequences for both the establishment and the underground press.

382. Costello, Donald P. "From Counterculture to Anticulture." *The Review of Politics* 34.4 (1972): 187–193. https://doi.org/10.1017/s0034670500021586

Claims three motion pictures both define and become participants of the 1960s counterculture: *Woodstock, Easy Rider,* and *A Clockwork Orange.* Suggests the movie *Woodstock* defined the counterculture by means of allowing the masses to experience the festival through "exploiting sights and sounds to a hyperrealism," thus providing both an ordered and intentionally chaotic perfection to the event. Observes 1960s culture was mostly communicated through sights and sounds rather than articulated through words. Offers as proof the film *Woodstock* as "perhaps the most verbally inarticulate film ever made." Continues by arguing *Woodstock* represents past values, *Easy Rider* deals with present [at the time this article was written] values, and *A Clockwork Orange* provides a glimpse of future values.

383. Goldstone, Bobbie. "Culture Vulture: Woodstock." *Off Our Backs* 1.6 (1970): 14.

Comments on the motion picture *Woodstock* from a feminist perspective. Observes that when viewing the film, one is aware of being manipulated into "responding in a pre-determined way to a pre-determined set of feelings and emotions." Comments on the portrayal of sex roles, with a focus on the way in which male sex objects are represented in film.

384. Kitts, Thomas M. "Documenting, Creating, and Interpreting Moments of Definition: 'Monterey Pop,' 'Woodstock,' and 'Gimme Shelter'." *Journal of Popular Culture* 42.4 (2009): 715–732. https://doi.org/10.1111/j.1540-5931.2009.00704.x

Demonstrates the ways in which the filmmakers of *Monterey Pop* (D. A. Pennebaker), *Woodstock* (Michael Wadleigh), and *Gimme Shelter* (Maysles brothers) edited their films to "document, create, interpret, and preserve" the mythologies associated with each music festival. Pennebaker celebrated the romantic, free-spirit, and innocence of the summer of 1967. Wadleigh revealed the tensions, contradictions, and ambiguities happening at the Woodstock Music and Art Fair in August 1969. Observes the Woodstock festival was a "very complex event with many nuanced, disconnected, and sometimes disparate occurrences." The motion picture *Woodstock* articulates this complexity and as a result both subverts and creates the Woodstock myth. Claims the Maysles brothers played upon the audiences' knowledge of the terrible events that occurred at the Altamont Speedway concert in late 1969 in order to "create the same sense of inexorable doom of a Greek tragedy." Views the three films as a trilogy, with an increasing presence of the filmmakers on the screen thus reflecting the changing culture towards the individual and away from the communal. Asserts when taken as a trilogy the films "provide an interpretive history of the rise and decline of the Sixties' counterculture spirit."

385. La Rosa, Melanie. "Early Video Pioneer: An Interview with Skip Blumberg." *Journal of Film and Video* 64.1–2 (2012): 30–41. https://doi.org/10.5406/jfilmvideo.64.1-2.0030

Interviews Skip Blumberg, a notable individual in the development of video documentary and experimental films. Responds to a question about the ways in which early video is now being utilized by referring to the Videofreex tapes made at the Woodstock Music and Art Fair. States these videos are "a detailed slice of what was happening behind the scenes" as opposed to the editorialized record of the motion picture *Woodstock*. Notes this unedited footage is being screened and appreciated for "the fresh and direct real-time experience" provided to the audience.

386. Messenger, Cory. "Record Collectors: Hollywood Record Labels in the 1950s and 1960s." *Media International Australia incorporating Culture and Policy* 148 (2013): 118–126.

Examines the evolution of film and music synergy which "transformed the marketing of recorded music, sparking a period of unprecedented commercial success for the record industry in the late 1960s." Presents the costs and profits behind both the motion picture *Woodstock* and the record album *Woodstock: Music from the Original Soundtrack and More*. Notes the Woodstock festival "represented the culmination of Hollywood's attempts to nurture a youth audience for film by drawing on methodologies developed within the rock music market." States Warner Bros. demonstrated the potential of cross-marketing between the film and music industries with the result being an upheaval in the "conventional methodologies of entertainment industry practice."

387. Plasketes, George M. "Rock on Reel: The Rise and Fall of the Rock Culture in America Reflected in a Decade of 'Rockumentaries'." *Qualitative Sociology* 12.1 (1989): 55–71. https://doi.org/10.1007/bf00989244

Analyzes the representation in motion pictures of American youth culture in the 1960s. Focuses on rockumentaries, including *Monterey Pop*, *Woodstock*, *Gimme Shelter*, and *The Last Waltz*. Explores "the ways in which popular film and music both reflect and define political and cultural movements" by means of "comparing and contrasting the plots and narrative techniques." Claims the 1960s was a time in which rock music captured and presented an alternate social order. Describes the motion picture *Woodstock* as resembling a romantic comedy. Observes the film "leaves the underlying impression that it does not completely share the spirit of the festival" and it's subjectivism lands somewhere between approval and criticism. Concludes with remarks on the evolution of rockumentaries from an emphasis on music to visuals of the music videos in the 1980s, transforming a music culture into a visual culture.

388. Reitinger, Douglas W. "Paint it Black: Rock Music and Vietnam War Film." *Journal of American Culture* 15.3 (1992): 53–59. https://doi.org/10.1111/j.1542-734x.1992.00053.x

Explores the use of rock music in Vietnam War films, specifically Francis Ford Coppola's *Apocalypse Now* and Stanley Kubrick's *Full Metal Jacket*. Introduces the article by contending the release of the motion picture *Woodstock* on two VHS videotapes altered the structure of the film "ultimately coloring any viewing or interpretation of it." Observes the first of the two tapes presents optimism and progressive cooperation (e.g., relationship building among various stakeholders) while the second tape shows a movement towards disaster and disillusionment (e.g., lack of sanitation, bad weather). Claims Woodstock as presented "symbolically and structurally in the video presentation" parallels the history of rock music and, specifically, its "nearly inseparable relationship with the Vietnam conflict."

389. Saunders, Dave. "Which Garden? Michael Wadleigh's Woodstock." *Vertigo* 3.5 (2007): 62–63. https://www.closeupfilmcentre.com/vertigo_magazine/volume-3-issue-5-spring-2007/which-garden-michael-wadleighs-woodstock/

Suggests a close examination of the motion picture *Woodstock* reveals more than a "finely composed memento" of the 1960s counterculture.

Highlights the balanced perspective represented in the film such that "for every utopian bliss there is an equal and opposite moment of dystopian misery." Notes the Woodstock festival only happened because of two catalysts: baby boomers and the Vietnam War. Contends the inherent theme of a fleeting idealized peacefulness marginalized by negative hedonism continues to be reinforced by anniversary concerts that "sully the dream."

390. Schowalter, Daniel F. "Remembering the Dangers of Rock and Roll: Toward a Historical Narrative of the Rock Festival." *Critical Studies in Media Communication* 17.1 (2000): 86–102. https://doi. org/10.1080/15295030009388377

Highlights the 1970 motion pictures *Woodstock* and *Gimme Shelter* to be representative of a historical narrative potentially promoting rock music as dangerous to society. Claims the *Woodstock* film focuses on the effects of music on the audience as opposed to the music itself. Editorial decisions served to de-politicize the festival by means of how it is documented in the final edit of the film. Makes similar observations regarding the *Gimme Shelter* film in that it is edited to document an interpretation of the event, in this case with a focus on audience violence. Insists the rock music narrative presented in the two motion pictures is clear, "it is but a small step for an enraptured and passive mass influenced by the sinister invisibility of rock music to become a violent and anesthetized mob." Introduces the motion picture *Monterey Pop* in order to expose the historical narrative of the other two motion pictures as being contrived because in its documenting of a music festival *Monterey Pop* focuses on the music as opposed to the effect on the audience. Concludes by warning viewers to be aware of the potential for documentaries to exploit representations and "inform political and moral argument."

391. Telotte, J. P. "Scorsese's 'The Last Waltz' and the Concert Genre." *Film Criticism* 4.2 (1980): 9–20.

Begins with a discussion of the movie musical genre and its inherent surrealism. Notes concert documentaries differ from other motion pictures within the genre because they show the natural world in which the music occurs. Points to both the films *Woodstock* and *Gimme Shelter* as being even further removed from the movie musical genre because "the activities of the concert-goers, the non-musical elements of the films, are given a heightened importance, effectively altering or enhancing our response to the music." Discourses on the motion picture *The Last Waltz* and how Martin Scorsese altered his editorial style used previously on *Woodstock* by crafting a self-enclosed environment for The

Band's last concert. Notes that rather than providing cameras shots from the audience and thus providing the viewer "the usual identification mechanism, he shoots nearly all of the actual concert footage from onstage."

392. Westrup, Laurel. "Medias Martyrs? Rock 'n' Roll, Film and the Political Economy of Death." *Spectator* 27 (2007): 33–41. https://cinema.usc.edu/assets/053/10907.pdf

Proposes the motion pictures *Woodstock* and *Gimme Shelter* (the infamous Altamont Speedway concert headlined by the Rolling Stones), both released in 1970 and each documenting a different 1969 rock concert, serve as "case studies that expose the role of death in the production, exhibition, and marketing of rock films." Discusses both films and their often juxtaposed themes (one celebrating life, the other documenting death) in the context of what the author describes as "the political economy of death." Analyzes various interpretations of the films as influenced by their marketing which has occurred over the years since they were first released.

Websites

393. Sobcynski, Peter. "Interview: Michael Wadleigh on 'Woodstock'." http://www.efilmcritic.com/feature.php?feature=2774

Interviews director Michael Wadleigh regarding his making of the motion picture *Woodstock*. Describes the film as one of the greatest documentaries ever produced. Claims without the movie the actual festival would be long forgotten. Wadleigh talks about how his previous work on the origins of the American Communist Party in Woodstock, New York, led to his involvement with the Woodstock Music and Art Fair. Articulates how it was decided which songs to film, given limited resources. Notes over 200 hours of footage were shot during the event. Asserts it is a myth some groups would not grant rights to be included in the motion picture and that the decisions on who to include were aesthetic. Concludes with Wadleigh explaining his lack of continued success as a filmmaker, noting his agenda was political and not artistic.

Videos

394. *Woodstock: 3 Days of Peace and Music (the Director's Cut).* Dir. Wadleigh, Michael. Warner Home Video, 2009

Documents to the fullest extent the entire three days of the Woodstock Music and Art Fair. Digitally remastered and includes two hours of never before seen footage, with five additional music acts (Paul Butterfield, Creedence Clearwater Revival, Grateful Dead, Mountain, Johnny Winter) not seen in any previous releases. Contains interviews with Michael Wadleigh (director), Martin Scorsese (editor), and Thelma Schoonmaker (editor). Maintains the frame mirroring, freeze frames, and multiple camera angles from the original 1970 theatrical release.

Arts & Literature

Books

395. Banes, Sally. *Terpsichore in Sneakers: Post-Modern Dance.* Middletown, CT: Wesleyan University Press, 1987.

Quotes choreographer Simone Forti explaining her inspirational experience at the Woodstock Music and Art Fair. She perceived a sharing of space and fate in a way that stimulated her to immerse herself into the hippie culture the following year.

396. Ertegun, Ahmet. *'What'd I Say': The Atlantic Story—50 Years of Music.* New York: Welcome Rain, 2001.

Presents the history of Ahmet Ertegun and Atlantic Records in an oversized coffee table book. Quotes Ertegun describing why he acquired the recording rights for the Woodstock Music and Art Fair, why he initially turned down the option to purchase the film rights, and how he eventually ended up with both. Includes glossy photographs from the festival.

397. Evans, Ron. *Chasing Woodstock: Finding the Cost of Freedom.* N. Clarendon, Vermont: Euprax Books, 2013.

Presents the results of the author's quest (i.e., *Woodstock Program Project*) to show Woodstock Music and Art Fair performers his copy of the long forgotten and rarely seen official program from the festival. Shares the musicians' "priceless and sometimes shocking" reactions. Provides insights not found elsewhere, but mostly serves as a light and entertaining read.

    http://dx.doi.org/10.11647/OBP.0105.06

398. *Grateful Dead: The Illustrated Trip*. New York: DK, 2003.

Serves as a coffee table book on the history of the Grateful Dead, arranged chronologically and illustrated extensively with color photographs. Describes the circumstances of the group's performance at the Woodstock Music and Art Fair. Notes their generally poor set at the festival and explains why they were not included in the motion picture *Woodstock*. Foreword by Robert Hunter.

399. Landy, Elliott. *Woodstock 1969: The First Festival*. Santa Rosa, CA: Squarebooks, 1994.

Presents a commemorative collection of both color and black and white photographs from the Woodstock Music and Art Fair. Contains images by a dozen photographers: Ralph Ackerman, Henry Diltz, Dan Garson, Charles Harbutt, Elliot Landy, Lisa Law, Barry Levine, Shelly Rusten, Peter Menzel, Joseph Sia, Burk Uzzle, and Baron Wolman. Includes reproductions of selected *New York Times* articles from the event. Provides contextual narratives from selected festival participants and photographers (John Roberts, John Morris, Lisa Law, Henry Diltz, Greil Marcus, Michael Lang, and Elliott Landy). Introduction by Jerry Garcia.

400. Landy, Elliott. *Woodstock Vision: The Spirit of a Generation*. New York: Continuum, 1994.

Collects photographs from the late 1960s taken by the author, a professional photographer. Devotes a section to the Woodstock Music and Art Fair. Includes an afterword by Richie Havens titled "The Essence of Woodstock" which he describes as "bringing people of like mind together." Havens claims that in 1994 "everyone now is a product of the Woodstock spirit."

401. Lang, Michael, Henry Diltz, and Dan Garson. *Woodstock Experience*. Guildford, U.K.: Genesis Publications, 2009.

Collects artifacts and other memorabilia related to the Woodstock Music and Art Fair. Packages photographs, art, graphics, recordings, and writings by Ben Fong-Torres, Dan Garson, Paul Krassner, George Lois and Tim O'Brien. Limited edition of 1,000 copies. Foreword by Arlo Guthrie.

402. Lawton, John. *Sweet Sunday*. New York: Atlantic Monthly Press, 2014.

Presents a work of fiction in which the protagonist, a private investigator, eventually attends the Woodstock Music and Art Fair.

403. Littleproud, Brad, and Joanne Hague. *Woodstock: Peace, Music &
Memories: 40th Anniversary.* Iola, WI: Krause, 2009.

Celebrates the 40th anniversary of the 1969 Woodstock Music and Art
Fair in a coffee table book format. Contains text of numerous personal
recollections from organizers, musicians, and attendees, along with
many color photographs. Reproduces newspaper articles, posters, and
other miscellaneous items (e.g., the contract used for hiring The Who).
Devotes one chapter to collecting memorabilia, with suggested items
and market values. Foreword by Artie Kornfeld, one of the Woodstock
organizers, and an epilogue by Wavy Gravy. Authors were members of
the Woodstock Preservation Alliance.

404. Logsdon, Gene. *The Mother of all Arts: Agrarianism and the Creative
Impulse.* Lexington, KY: University Press of Kentucky, 2007. https://doi.
org/10.5810/kentucky/9780813124438.001.0001

Studies the way in which "the creative impulse in art acts itself out when
influenced by farming and rural life." Explores connections between art
and agriculture and the impact on society. Claims, in a chapter titled
"Singing Farmers," the massive turnout of urbanites to the Woodstock
Music and Art Fair was a desire to discover "primeval agrarian roots,
instinctively, if not consciously." Asserts that above all else, the festival
was "an example of how art could be profoundly influenced by old
mother agriculture, even if in a pathetic way." Suggests the concert
was a trigger event for the back-to-the-land movement that became
predominant among members of the counterculture.

405. *Rosebud: Jenny Holzer, Matt Mullican, Lawrence Weiner.* Eds.
Michael Tarantino and Ulrich Wilmes. Munich, Germany: Kunstbau
Lenbachhaus München, 1994.

Serves as an exhibition catalogue for a touring set of installations by
American artists Jenny Holzer, Matt Mullican and Lawrence Weiner.
The section of text by Ulrich Wilmes uses two culmination events
from 1969, the Apollo moon landing and the Woodstock Music and
Art Fair, to proclaim the reality of art is determined by its relationship
to the present. Suggests that art "conveys an aesthetic experience of
reality whose authenticity is a function of permanent progress" in the
conditions of its making. Considers the impact of this on avant-garde
art and the possibility of it becoming "an emancipatory model for the
self-identification of the individual in relation to others."

406. Sackett, Linanne G., and Barry Z. Levine. *The Woodstock Story Book: A Chronologically and Anatomically Correct Illustrated Tale for Post-Woodstock Generations.* Troy, NY: Brunswick Institute, 2009.

> Publishes nearly 300 large color photographs accompanied by text written in child's verse, but clearly intended as an adult story book. Photographer Barry Z. Levine was part of the *Woodstock* film crew and captured the event with his camera on site prior to, during, and after the August 1969 weekend of the festival. Reproduces the lyrics to *I-Feel-Like-I'm-Fixing-To-Die Rag* by Country Joe McDonald. Contains a foreword by Wavy Gravy, who states the book "brings back for me the magic that was Woodstock—the energy of the community that terrified the powers that be." Includes photographs taken at the concert identifying members of the film crew and, more recently, a photograph of the commemorative monument at the site. Concludes with an afterword by the photographer reflecting back on the 1969 festival.

407. Sia, Joseph J. *Woodstock 69: Summer Pop Festivals.* New York: Scholastic Book Services, 1970.

> Collects black and white photographs of audiences and performers from selected major music festivals held in 1969, from the Newport Jazz Festival to the Woodstock Music and Art Fair. Many of the musicians appearing at Woodstock also performed at a number of these other music festivals. Observes that even though dire predictions were made about potential violence and crisis-like conditions at such a large gathering as Woodstock, attendees simply came to "listen to the supersounds of their favorite rock groups." Paperback quality printing.

408. Soares, Valérie I. O., and Jack Tzekov. *Lily and Kayden's 1969 Woodstock Adventure.* Ottawa, Canada: Petra Books, 2014.

> Children's book about two youngsters taken on a flying couch to the Woodstock Music and Art Fair.

409. Sonnenblick, Jordan. *Are You Experienced?* New York: Feiwel and Friends, 2013.

> Presents young adult fiction in which a contemporary fifteen-year-old boy is transported back in time to the Woodstock Music and Art Fair.

410. Tiber, Elliot. *Woodstock Delirium: Music, Mayhem & Madness.* New York: Woodstock Delirium, 2001.

> Represents a humorous "fictionalized version of non-fiction events." Foreword by Richie Havens.

411. Wallace, Rich. *War & Watermelon*. New York: Puffin Books, 2012.

Presents a young adult fictional coming of age story in which the twelve year old main character attends the 1969 Woodstock Music and Art Fair.

412. Walter, Greg, and Lisa Grant. *Woodstock: A New Look*. Cranston, RI: Writers Collective, 2008.

Presents the author's personal photographs mixed with those from the Associated Press and Henry Diltz, all taken during the 1969 Woodstock Music and Art Fair. Explains Walter was eighteen years of age and an employee of Woodstock Ventures. Notes he was hired to work on the art crew and he helped to build the stage. Describes the process by which he was hired, his meeting Max Yasgur, and his experiences during the three days of the concert. During his time before and while at the festival, the author took lots of photographs, developed them as slides, and then forgot about them for forty years. Thus, this work includes many photographs of the event not previously seen by anyone. Uses the Afterword to describe the author's experience as a Vietnam War draft dodger.

413. Westfahl, Gary. *William Gibson*. Urbana, IL: University of Illinois Press, 2013.

Relates very briefly William Gibson, science fiction author, describing his experience at the Woodstock Music and Art Fair as being "like going to a Civil War battle."

414. Wolman, Baron. *Woodstock*. London: Reel Art Press, 2014.

Collects scores of black and white photographs taken by Baron Wolman at the Woodstock Music and Art Fair in 1969. Concentrates on images of the throngs of festival attendees. Notes how Wolman "was fascinated, captivated, enchanted and transfixed by the crowd." Transcribes a lengthy joint interview with Wolman and Michael Lang (one of the Woodstock promoters), conducted by Dagon James. Quotes Wolman describing how he and photographer Jim Marshall had spent the summer of 1969 traveling the country photographing music festivals. Delves into many detailed aspects of the Woodstock festival and its aftermath. Reproduces as an appendix Wolman's contact sheets from the event. Includes a Foreword by Carlos Santana.

415. *Woodstock '94: The Book*. New York: Callaway Editions, 1994.

Commemorates the Woodstock '94 concert. Gathers both color and black and white photographs interspersed with text in the style of an exhibition catalog. Includes black and white backstage portraits of performers and audience photographs taken by Albert Watson. Contains essays by John Milward and Christopher John Farley. Foreword by Amy Wu.

416. Yasgur, Abigail, and Joseph Lipner. *Max Said Yes!: The Woodstock Story.* Los Angeles: Change the Universe Press, 2009.

Presents a child's story book, included here as an artifact. One of the co-authors is a relative of Max Yasgur. Quotes Max Yasgur's edited remarks from the stage at the Woodstock Music and Art Fair. Includes the lyrics to Joni Mitchell's song *Woodstock.* Illustrated by Barbara Mendes.

Chapters

417. Burt, Ramsay. "Simone Forti and Bill T. Jones at Woodstock." *Judson Dance Theater: Performative Traces.* London: Routledge, 2006. 130–134. https://doi.org/10.4324/9780203969663

Explores the development and legacy of the Judson Dance Theater in the creation of postmodern dance. Contrasts two differing race-based perspectives on the avant-garde by using personal narratives of individual experiences from the Woodstock Music and Art Fair. Criticizes Forti for believing her observations of an African-American attendee dancing represented "an ahistorical, premodern past." Suggests she is naive for not considering the experience from the dancer's perspective. Observes Jones' description of an audience member (his brother) dancing is "both personal and political," noting this possibility had not occurred to Forti.

418. Chess, Richard. "Alan Shapiro (1952-)." *Holocaust Literature: An Encyclopedia of Writers and their Work.* Ed. S. Lillian Kremer. New York: Routledge, 2003. 1152–1155.

Discusses a poem about the Holocaust titled "Mud Dancing" and set at the 1969 Woodstock Music and Art Fair. Notes the poem "invokes the ghosts of victims of the Holocaust who are drawn to the scene because of its familiarity."

419. Cooke, Jon B. "Still Chaykin After all these Years: A Life in American Comics." *Howard Chaykin: Conversations.* Ed. Brannon Costello. Jackson, MS: University Press of Mississippi, 2011. 188–241.

Quotes Howard Chaykin (noted comic book writer, artist, and graphic novel pioneer) explaining his Woodstock Music and Art Fair experience.

States he went to the festival in a '63 Bonneville convertible and once there he learned "I don't do dirty and smelly well." Reprinted from *Comic Book Artist.* v. 2, no. 5 (December 2004). The rest of the book reveals Chaykin's aesthetics through a series of other reprinted interviews.

420. Dolin, Sharon. "Phonography." *Whirlwind.* Pittsburgh, PA: University of Pittsburgh Press, 2012. 57.

Presents a collection of the author's poems, including "Phonography" in which playing the record album *Woodstock: Music from the Original Soundtrack and More* evokes childhood memories of the Vietnam War.

421. "Flashbacks." *1969: Woodstock, the Moon and Manson: The Turbulent End of the '60s.* Ed. Kelly Knauer. New York: Time Books, 2009. 88–93.

Presents a photographic essay on the Woodstock Music and Art Fair using both color and black and white photographs of the performers and audience.

422. Forti, Simone. "The Garden." *Handbook in Motion.* Halifax, Canada: The Press of Nova Scotia College of Art and Design, 1974. 15–16. https://monoskop.org/images/4/4e/Forti_Simone_Handbook_in_Motion.pdf

Collects drawings, photographs, essays, and handwritten notes by Forti, a dancer, choreographer, and musician. Recounts her experience attending the Woodstock Music and Art Fair. Describes dancing to her simultaneous hearing of various pockets of music "already somewhat integrated because they were within earshot of each other." Remembers feeling a shared ethos of space and fate.

Articles

423. Dumas, Timothy. "Still Together Now." *Smithsonian* 40.5 (2009): 6–8.

Reveals how the photograph used for the iconic *Woodstock: Music from the Original Soundtrack and More* album came to be taken. Notes the picture is of a couple (Nick Ercoline and Bobbi Kelly) embracing at the festival. Describes the journey that randomly brought together the photographer (Burk Uzzle) and the subjects at the right moment in time to capture a candid image representing the peace and love ethos of the event. Reveals the significance of the plastic butterfly also capture in the image. Explains "a spaced-out Californian named Herbie tagged along, carrying a wooden staff with a plastic butterfly dancing from the tip." Adds he had joined Ercoline and Kelly on their walking trek to the festival after having abandoned their Impala station wagon along the way. Notes the famous photograph was taken as Jefferson Airplane played in the dawn's early light.

424. Ecker, David W. "The Structure of Affect in the Art Curriculum." *Art Education* 24.1 (1971): 26–29. https://doi.org/10.2307/3191570

Calls for a re-examination of art curriculum "in terms of the relationship between the affective and cognitive structures now built into it and those structures our students display outside of school," meaning the 1960s counterculture ethos. Uses descriptions by attendees of the Woodstock Music and Art to illustrate the "structure of affect." Recommends art educators better understand student attitudes, feelings, values, and beliefs and how these things should be discussed in the classroom as learning objectives. Offers art curriculum should be open ended. Contends "deeply felt experiences both of the creative process and the aesthetic response to art should be the overall objective of art education."

425. Hafen, P. Jane. "Rock and Roll, Redskins, and Blues in Sherman Alexie's Work." *Studies in American Indian Literatures* 9.4 (1997): 71–78.

Discusses the writings of Sherman Alexie as being "a fusion of historical sensibilities and grim realisms of contemporary Indian life." Describes a chapter from Alexie's book *The Lone Ranger and Tonto Fistfight in Heaven* in which the Woodstock Music and Art Fair is used to manifest the hippie movement's affectation of American Indian culture, one which does not symbolize counterculture subversion but instead becomes "merely another extension of colonialism." Relays the deep affinity the narrator's father had for Jimi Hendrix. Suggests the challenge for critics assessing the works of Alexie is to assess his body of work "in terms of tribal and intellectual sovereignty."

426. Hernandez, Debra Gersh. "No Nudes is Good Nudes: Firs-Prize Photograph in the White House News Photographers Association Competition Creates a Stir." *Editor and Publisher* 128.6 (1995): 9–10.

Relays the story of a photograph taken by Kenneth Lambert at Woodstock '94 depicting a naked man sitting in a lawn chair with a woman looking at him cynically. Highlights the photograph's award of first prize in a White House News Photographers Association (WHNPA) competition. States the photographer wanted to illustrate how the festival differed from the original Woodstock Music and Art Fair because the male subject is the only person naked and is being shown some disdain by others at the event. Notes an unsuccessful attempt by Ken Blaylock to ban the photograph from an exhibition and publication for being "inappropriate."

427. Hirsch, Edward. "The Duende." *American Poetry Review* 28.4 (1999): 13–21.

Contemplates Federico Garcia Lorca's invocation of the Dionysian spirit of art as *duende*. Describes Lorca's definition of *duende* as "not a completed work in and of itself, but a force that drives through the work, that electrifies it." Explores the presence of *duende* in modern American art. Illustrates the essence of *duende* through examples, including Jimi Hendrix's performance of *The Star Spangled Banner* at the Woodstock Music and Art Fair. Offers the rendering "reverberated across the fields with the gusto of an American childhood, with the patriotic memory of previous American wars, with the flaming sounds of an undeclared war going on halfway across the world." Includes a poetic description of Hendrix's performance by James McManus. Compares Hendrix's description of his version of the national anthem to vernacular "heard often in the dark personal agon of our poetry." Concludes by describing *duende*, in part, as "a joy that burns and a suffering that scalds."

428. Hoberman, J. "Moon Dance: On the Summer of '69." *Artforum International* 32.10 (1994): 10, 117.

Compares and contrasts two major events from 1969 as being two of the most culturally significant events of the twentieth century: the Apollo moon launch in July and the Woodstock Music and Art Fair in August. Interjects the occurrences of the Manson murders and other major news items from that year.

429. Meyer, James. "Impure Thoughts: The Art of Sam Durant." *Artforum International* 38.8 (2000): 112–117.

Profiles American artist Sam Durant, whose installation *Partially Buried 1960s/70s: Utopia Reflected, Dystopia Revealed* (1998) builds upon the dichotomous relationship between the Woodstock Music and Art Fair and Altamont Speedway concert, both of 1969. Explores the "dialectical relationship of the two, the entropic collapse of one state into another." Dissects the mythology surround the juxtaposed events to demonstrate a "basic structural logic."

430. Rohlehr, F. G. "Some Problems of Assessment: A Look at New Expressions in the Arts of the Contemporary Caribbean." *Caribbean Quarterly* 17.3/4 (1971): 92–113.

> Mentions in a few words the impact of the motion picture *Woodstock* on Trinidad in the early 1970s. Claims the film's "white liberal orientation and vagueness, its atmosphere of cliché and escapism, provided the youth with all the justification that they needed for a retreat into the uneasy nirvana of weed and pills."

431. Schwartz, Steven. "What We Talk About When We Talk about Negative Attachment." *The North American Review* 290.2 (2005): 43–52.

> Presents a short fiction in which a trip in 1969 to the Woodstock Music and Art Fair is included.

432. Shapiro, Alan. "Woodstock Puritan." *TriQuarterly* 92 (1994): 139–164.

> Presents a story recounting coming of age in the era of the 1960's counterculture. Ponders on the narrator's experiences as reflected from his close friend's social and political transformation. Describes their pilgrimage to the Woodstock Music and Art Fair in August 1969 as having reached the promised land, at least initially. Observes how at the event "we could openly do with no fear of reprisal what we had grown accustomed to doing late at night behind locked doors." Comments in some detail on the two's experience of surviving the weekend at the festival while at the same time growing apart.

433. Snaevarr, Stefan. "Dylan as a Rortian: Bob Dylan, Richard Rorty, Postmodernism, and Political Skepticism." *Journal of Aesthetic Education* 48.4 (2014): 38–49. https://doi.org/10.5406/jaesteduc.48.4.0038

> Examines Bob Dylan's postmodern political skepticism as expressed in his music and writings dating from the 1960s. Introduces Richard Rorty's philosophy to ground the essay in theory. Invokes Jimi Hendrix's performance of *The Star Spangled Banner* at the Woodstock Music and Art Fair as an example of music expressing political emotions. Claims Hendrix's rendering the piece without words messaged the patriotic lyrics as being near worthless. Suggests Hendrix demonstrated how one can articulate political emotions using nonverbal symbols. Concludes by stating Dylan "uses artistic means" to create a political multidimensional dialogue avoiding traditional dichotomies.

434. Sussler, Betsy. "James McLure." *BOMB* 5 (1983): 32–34. http://bombmagazine.org/article/234/james-mclure

Prints an interview with James McLure discussing, among other things, his play *The Day They Shot John Lennon* which includes two characters who had attended at the Woodstock Music and Art Fair. Contrasts their reactions to John Lennon's murder with those reactions of the other characters.

435. "Woodstock Music Festival." *Aperture* 107 (1987): 56.

Reproduces a photograph taken by Jason Laure at the 1969 Woodstock Music and Art Fair in a thematic issue titled "Mothers & Daughters: That Special Quality."

436. Young, Julian. "Artwork and Sportwork: Heideggerian Reflections." *Journal of Aesthetics and Art Criticism* 57.2 (1999): 267–277. https://doi.org/10.2307/432318

Theorizes Martin Heidegger's "principal paradigm of the artwork is more illuminating with respect to modern sport than it is with respect to modern art." Evokes the Woodstock Music and Art Fair as an alleged Heideggerian artwork, but acknowledges it was "a barren event" without successors, making it a "reactive phenomenon, a protest against the way of life that had led to the Vietnam war rather than the positive affirmation of the integrity of any, even subcultural, community." Proclaims sporting events are better representations of Heideggerian artwork because of the coming together of players and spectators into a large group consisting of a wide societal cross-section.

Websites

437. Brau, Edgar. "Woodstock." 2007. http://wordswithoutborders.org/article/woodstock

Offers a poem by the Argentine author, translated by Michael McKay Aynesworth.

Authors, Editors and Directors Index

Authors, editors, and directors of items cited in this work are listed. Numbers following the names are the citation entry numbers, not page numbers.

Subject Index

This is a detailed subject index to the relevant contents of the works cited, not just to the annotations. Numbers following the subjects are the citation entry numbers, not page numbers.

This book need not end here...

At Open Book Publishers, we are changing the nature of the traditional academic book. The title you have just read will not be left on a library shelf, but will be accessed online by hundreds of readers each month across the globe. OBP publishes only the best academic work: each title passes through a rigorous peer-review process. We make all our books free to read online so that students, researchers and members of the public who can't afford a printed edition will have access to the same ideas.

This book and additional content is available at:
http://www.openbookpublishers.com/isbn/9781783742882

Customize

Personalize your copy of this book or design new books using OBP and third-party material. Take chapters or whole books from our published list and make a special edition, a new anthology or an illuminating coursepack. Each customized edition will be produced as a paperback and a downloadable PDF. Find out more at:

http://www.openbookpublishers.com/section/59/1

Donate

If you enjoyed this book, and feel that research like this should be available to all readers, regardless of their income, please think about donating to us. We do not operate for profit and all donations, as with all other revenue we generate, will be used to finance new Open Access publications.

http://www.openbookpublishers.com/section/13/1/support-us

Like Open Book Publishers **f**

Follow @OpenBookPublish **y**

Read more at the Open Book Publishers **BLOG**

www.ingramcontent.com/pod-product-compliance
Lightning Source LLC
Chambersburg PA
CBHW061737270326
41928CB00011B/2275